CHILD DEVELOPMENT: ANALYSIS AND SYNTHESIS

by

JOSEPH H. DI LEO, M. D.

Routledge
Taylor & Francis Group
LONDON AND NEW YORK

CHILD DEVELOPMENT: ANALYSIS AND SYNTHESIS

First published 1977 by Brunner/Mazel, Inc.

Published 2022 by Routledge
2 Park Square, Milton Park, Abingdon, Oxon OX14 4RN
605 Third Avenue, New York, NY 10017

Routledge is an imprint of the Taylor & Francis Group, an informa business

First issued in hardback 2016

Library of Congress Cataloging in Publication Data

Di Leo, Joseph H 1902–1994
Child development

Bibliography: p. 168
Includes indexes.
1. Child psychology. I. Title. [DNLM: 1. Child development. 2. Creativeness.
WS103 D576c]
BF721.D54 155.4 77-5381
ISBN 0-87630-141-3
Paperback edition 1996 ISBN: 0-87630-834-5

ISBN 978-0-87630-834-9 (pbk)
ISBN 978-1-138-16129-0 (hbk)

Contents

Introduction

Many years ago, in the course of my residency in pediatrics, it became increasingly clear to me that what I was learning about formulas, immunizations, and disease was pitifully little about what really mattered—the child. Quite by chance, I came upon a volume that was to mark a turning point in my career—*Developmental Diagnosis* by Gesell and Amatruda, in which were described the changing patterns of behavior as the child matured during the first three years. It was utterly fascinating and opened up a whole new horizon. Later, when the opportunity arose to go to the Yale Clinic of Child Development, I responded enthusiastically. There, under the direction of Gesell and Amatruda, I was trained in the techniques of developmental evaluation.

After this training, I was charged with the direction of a clinic for the appraisal of growth and development at the New York Foundling Hospital. I have continued in that capacity these thirty odd years. It soon became apparent, however, that the observation, recording, and conclusions drawn from the developmental evaluations left many questions unanswered. To fill in the gaps, I added to the technique a neurological survey aimed at determining the absence or persistence of certain reflexes peculiar to the developing organism. But it seemed that we must also consider the adverse environmental factors, and the inhibitions and disorders of motility so common in infants without families. I found help in Anna Freud's writings on children separated from their families. Erikson's classic, *Childhood and Society,* added a social dimension to the comprehensive view I was developing.

Piaget's monumental work on how children learn added an indispensable aspect to what was now an almost total view. My interest and study of drawings by young children provided an opportunity to see what children thought and felt about people and themselves.

No one could be expected in a lifetime to investigate the whole and its complexity. But drawing from the masters, as well as my own clinical experience, might it not be possible to view the whole synoptically? There is no other valid way. It must be done if we are to help the child and not merely one part. The reality is that the parts do not exist as such. Body, physiology, intellect, emotions, and experience are inseparable aspects of a whole. The subject of our study is an integrated whole. Difficult as it may be, the child cannot be understood unless the aspects mentioned, as well as others which may be relevant, are taken into account. With this end in view, I shall first briefly survey each aspect singly, then show how they are interrelated, and finally present a synoptic chart that illustrates not only the time relationship but also the oneness of the subject under consideration. Having found this effort most helpful, I am offering it to those working with children as a practical device for keeping the forest in mind while examining the trees.

Before attempting to present the various aspects of development in a stage-to-stage relationship, I shall review in outline those stage-dependent theories that I believe to be the most coherent, having found them the most helpful in my long association with children and their problems.

Psychoanalytic theory as presented in the work of S. Freud, A. Freud, M. Mahler and R. Spitz, provides the framework for the outline of affective development. Its application to social development is derived from E. Erikson. Cognitive developmental stages are those of J. Piaget. For the outline of behavior patterns based on decades of systematic observation, I have turned to A. Gesell. The sequences in drawing behavior, in which cognition and affect fuse, are as identified by G. H. Luquet in his pioneer observations and interpretations and as described in my own publications. Language developmental stages are based on the work of McCarthy, Gesell, Brown, Myklebust, Lenneberg, and others.

Some, but perhaps not all, of these outlines will seem superfluous to those who are familiar with the theories from which the survey is derived. To others, the outlines may stimulate a desire for more substance, which they will find in the list of selected references.

The book is divided into three sections. In the first, the world of childhood is viewed, described, investigated, and interpreted by adults. In the second, the children speak for themselves. In word, and more cogently in deed, they tell of themselves and of the adults who constitute their world. The third section is devoted to a synthesis of views that are often in only apparent conflict.

The child who is known only through adults is known wrong.

PART ONE

The World of Childhood as Seen by Adults

1

DEVELOPMENTAL STAGES

All development is a continuous process. There are no exceptions to this rule. It applies to psychological as well as biological development. Yet, even in its physical aspects, there are differences in the pattern of growth: The brain takes an early lead while genital maturation lags far behind; rapid spurts in general body growth occur during the first and preadolescent years; qualitative as well as quantitative changes transform the child into an adult. The child is not a miniature adult.

Cognitive, psychosexual, psychosocial, and even drawing behavior displays no exceptions to the phenomenon of lawful growth. Development proceeds stage by stage in orderly sequence, and although there are individual variations, these do not basically alter the ground plan that is typical of our species and that, inherent in the DNA of our first 46 chromosomes, distinguishes us from all other forms of life.

Development sometimes takes a quantum jump but, like all biological phenomena, it is a continuum. It advances upward and forward, not in linear fashion, but more like a spiral, with its downward as well as upward cycle, yet always a bit more upward and a bit less downward, each stage representing a level of maturity whose features are qualitatively different yet derived from and dependent upon the earlier stages.

It is within this conceptual framework of identifiable stages in the developmental continuum that I shall attempt to show the relationships that express the oneness of the organism and the unifying concept of growth.

2

CRITICAL PERIODS

The theory of critical periods has gained support from phenomena observed in biological development and from clinical observations in the behavioral sciences.

There can be no doubt that in embryological development timing plays a crucial role. The effects of noxious exogenous agents on embryonic differentiation are influenced by the timing of the insult. The role of sensitive periods in teratogenesis is beyond question: The thalidomide disaster is a dramatic case in point. The effects of cosmic radiation, viruses, pollutants, and drugs are clearly related to the time of their action during organogenesis, as well as to the specific noxious agent. The first prenatal months are a time of particular vulnerability, for it is during this period that arms, and eyes, and lips, and brains may be arrested and deformed. Animal experiments have demonstrated impaired brains due to unavailability of essential nutrients during the late prenatal and early neonatal period. Studies of deprived human populations suggest the possibility of impaired intellectual functioning in children who suffered from similar early malnutrition. More specifically, studies of neural development in mammals indicate the need for specific proteins and lipids at the right time for normal growth of the myelin sheath that insulates nerve fibres. Critical periods have been detected in the stages of neural proliferation and dendritic formation.

How neural structure affects behavior is a fascinating problem under continual investigation. The weight of evidence supports the view that once a system becomes organized it resists reorganization (Scott, 1962). This principle applies to structure and to function. There are optimal periods for physical growth and there is considerable clinical evidence that there are sensitive periods for behavioral development, for learning, and for the acquisition of social skills. The conviction that such sensitive periods do actually occur has drawn attention to the abiding effects of one's earliest encounters with environmental influences and, crucially, of exchanges between child and nurturing adult.

The concept of critical periods has far-reaching implications for the care, education, and training of children, as well as for their physical health and well-being.

Rene Spitz has stressed the critical significance of three periods in the early development of the psyche. During these periods, "organizers" of the psyche are established. The first of these organizers is the smiling response, which appears at about six weeks. At first indiscriminate, responding to any nodding full-face, the social smile is gradually directed more to the mothering person. A second organizer is represented by the anxiety which is often displayed at about eight months, when the infant reacts negatively to strangers and shows a decided preference for the mother figure. She has become the established libidinal object in whom the infant's aggressive and affective drives are fused. During the second year, the third organizer is represented by the words *no, nein, niet,* and by the ubiquitous horizontal shaking of the head that universally expresses negation and the awareness of a separate and distinct self.

Studies of animal psychology, notably by Konrad Lorenz, indicate that the critical period for imprinting in animals occurs soon after birth. By waddling and quacking like a mallard mother, newly-hatched ducklings took him on as their mother, following and responding to him in typical duckling fashion. In humans, it is suggested that the critical period for "imprinting," that is, for the establishment of the libidinal object, occupies a much longer period and requires reciprocally gratifying tactile, auditory, visual, and emotional interaction.

Establishment of the gender role in human beings is not a function of chromosomal sex, gonadal sex, or hormones, and although the character of the external genitalia does play a role, it is not necessarily a determining one. Environmental factors are involved and often play a decisive role. These environmental influences operating early in life may result in the assumption of a sexual orientation that is at variance with the biological sex. Clinical evidence places the critical period for gender role and orientation well within the preschool years.

3

THE NEURAL SUBSTRATE

Underlying all behavioral development is the maturation of the nervous system. The repertory of patterned reflexes that is present in the newborn is based on changes in the structure of the nervous system that have been going on long before birth. The gradual weakening and eventual disappearance of these phylogenetic reflexes coincide with the descent of moderating and controlling influences from the supra-segmental hierarchical structures. "The direction of development is cephalocaudad. The first movable parts to come under volitional control are those nearest the brain, namely, the eyes. Thence forward, progressively downward and distally into the extremities, controlled movements occur until mastery is established over the skeletal musculature and even over emotional expression. Meanwhile, growing awareness and accumulating experience are making sensory reception increasingly meaningful and elevating it to the level of perception. . . . The persistence of certain phylogenetic reflexes beyond the time that they should have disappeared is a sign of delayed encephalization of behavior or of damage to the central nervous system" (Di Leo, 1967). Among the reflexes destined to extinction during the normal course of development are the Moro, tonic-neck reflex, indiscriminate sucking, automatic hand grasp and toe grasp, and Babinski.

As behavior evolves, structural maturation proceeds at a continuous, progressive pace. During the fetal period, the brain takes an early lead and outstrips all other systems in rapidity and complexity of growth and maturation. Histologically, the changes are revealed as a striking proliferation of brain cells and a differentiation of the cortex into layers.

At birth, the brain is by far the most developmentally advanced organ in the body. Its average weight (350 grams) is one-fourth of the weight of an adult brain. The male brain is slightly heavier than the female's, but this is not associated with a functional advantage. Already, at birth, the brain has its full complement of neurons—approximately 10 billion—as well as the nerve cells of the rest of the nervous system. The only cells that are added are the neuroglia; these are the supporting structures of the nervous system. Neurons begin to die in early adulthood. By age 35, approximately 100,000 brain cells are lost every day (Crelin, 1973). (This is just one of the indications that the human organism reaches its peak efficiency during adolescence.)

In the newborn, function is mediated from the midbrain. Though all neurons that one will ever have are present in the cortex, the nerve fibres (axons) issuing from the cell bodies are not efficiently conducting impulses. To do so, the axons must first acquire their myelin sheath, a process that proceeds distally from the cell body. Only then can the cortical cells exert their controlling, moderating influence over the phylogenetically older subcortical system that blindly governs the diffuse, reflex activity of the newborn. Descending control by the cortex is largely inhibitory and is manifested by restriction of response and gradual disappearance of the blind, inborn, atavistic reflexes (rooting, automatic hand and toe grasp, stepping, Moro, doll's eyes, tonic-neck reflex).

Inhibitory control from the cortex is an essential prerequisite for the emergence of voluntary, goal-directed response. As this is occurring, the electroencephalogram shows the appearance of alpha-type 3 per second rhythm.

As myelination and control spread downward and distally

into the face, trunk, and limbs, voluntary movements replace the generalized responses of the immature organism. The response to stimuli from eyes, ears, skin, and muscles becomes increasingly appropriate. The infant thinks motorically. Piaget calls this the sensori-motor stage. Freud called it the oral stage, for everything is experienced with the mouth, currently the prime organ for pleasurable, sensitive contact with an object, living or inanimate. Touch and movement are intimately interwoven in structure and function, in the brain and in action. The mouth and the finger must move in order to feel. In the brain, the motor area has sensory elements, while the sensory area has motoric elements.

By age three the brain has attained three-quarters of its adult weight. By age five, it will have attained 90 percent of its adult size. Its capacity for storage and retrieval is impressive. As the child achieves mastery over the action system, movements will become effortless, as they are almost unconsciously performed in the service of purpose and goal. The child is then free to explore the environment as boundaries are enlarged and curiosity and assertiveness become dominant traits . . . unless physical or environmentally imposed restrictions create deviations in the normal flow of development.

During prenatal development, spontaneous movements occur as early as three weeks, when the heart begins its lifelong beat. Response to stimulation of the mouth region has been noted in the two-month embryo. Spontaneous movements of the total organism have been noted as early as nine weeks. As the fifth-month fetus becomes increasingly active, the mother becomes aware of a life within her. The full repertory of phylogenetic patterned reflexes typical of the full-term newborn is already present in the seventh-month fetus; these include the Moro, suspension grasp, rooting, sucking, toe grasp, and Babinski reflexes. Underlying these manifestations is the structural-functional maturation of the central and peripheral neural apparatus, in which enzymatic, endocrine, electrical, and other physio-chemical phenomena play a correlative, as yet imperfectly understood, role.

Considerable insight into the activity of the nervous system even before birth is provided by electroencephalographic studies. Brain waves reaching the surface of the cortex have been detected as early as the seventh fetal month. Using the electroencephalogram as an index of maturation, stages have been defined in the steady progression from the earliest fetal recording to the adult pattern. In this continuum, qualitative changes in brain waves coincide with observed functional changes.

Prior to the eighth fetal month, EEG activity is disorganized; each hemisphere seems to be functioning independently of the other, and there is no difference between waking and sleeping patterns. By the eighth fetal month, voltage increases and there is a suggestion of differentiation between waking and sleeping states, as well as an indication of interdependence between hemispheres.

Lindsley (1936) studied the EEG record of 100 children ranging in age from one month to 16 years. The records were obtained from the occipital region of the brain in which the visual area is located. Before the age of three months, brain waves were irregular, and no rhythmic activity was seen. Shortly after three months, brief rhythmic alpha-type sequences were noted. Concomitantly, the infant was making the first volitionally-directed movements: those of the eyes in pursuit of a moving object. The onset of rhythmic activity in the EEG record appears to be associated with functional activity of the brain. The difference between waking and sleeping states is also beginning to be defined at this time, as sleep spindles appear in the record.

Another interesting fact that emerged from the study was the gradual increase in frequency of the rhythmic alpha-type activity with age. Starting with an average frequency of 3.8 per second at three months, the increase was consistent and uniform, reaching a maximum frequency of 11.2 per second at age 10. Lindsley cautiously stated that the progressive upward trend "suggests a developmental process of some sort." The frequency at age 10 to 12 is somewhat higher than the average of 10.4 in adults and may express the physiological changes that are occurring at that developmental period of rapid growth and approaching puberty.

Figure 1 shows the normal encephalographic record of a 15-year-old boy. The three EEG tracings in Figures 2, 3 and 4 illustrate the changes that occur as a six-year-old child progresses into deep sleep. As the child falls into deeper sleep, there is an inverse correlation between amplitude and frequency.

The two hemispheres of the brain are in communication with each other through the corpus callosum. Their function, however, is not identical. It has long been known that the right hemisphere controls the volitional movements of the left side of

FIGURE 1

In this encephalographic record may be seen the normal adult pattern of 10 c.p.s. alpha rhythmic activity, which is established by the twelfth year.

The 3 EEG tracings that follow illustrate the changes that occur as the six-year-old child progresses into deep sleep.

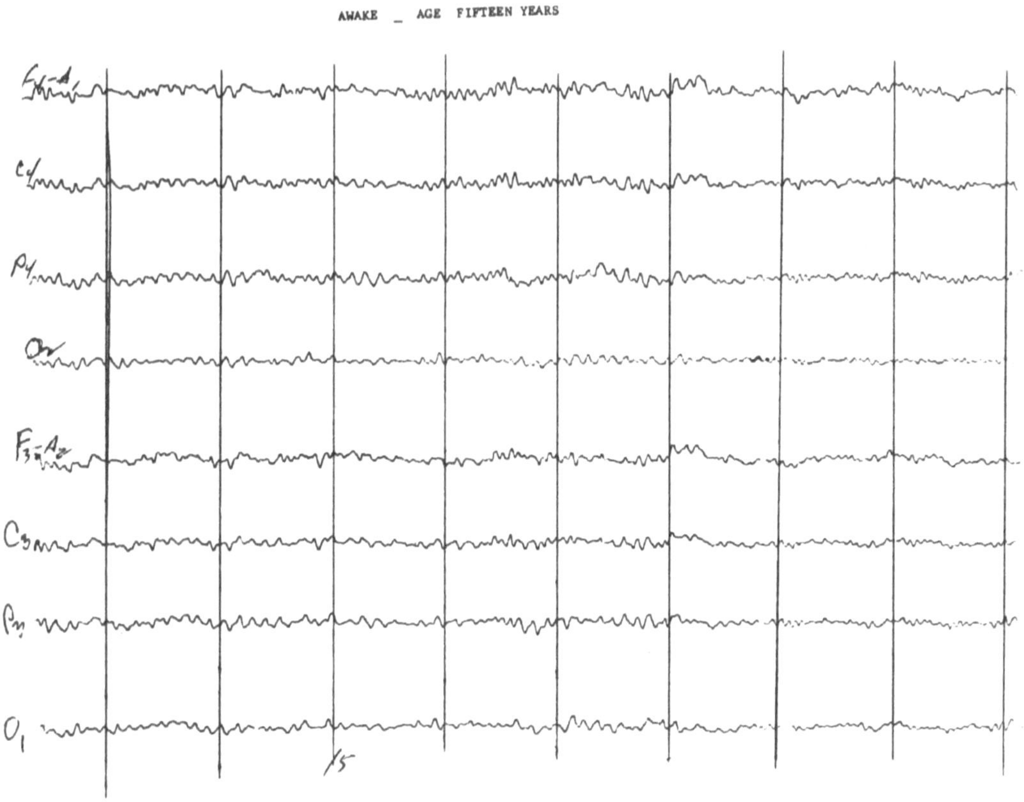

the body, and vice versa. Further, the main speech area is located in the left hemisphere in most persons, so that damage to that side of the cerebral cortex is likely to result in aphasia. Sensations from various parts of the body reach consciousness when transmitted to the sensory area on the opposite side of the brain.

But beyond these hard facts, recent research is attributing more specific functions at higher levels of integration to each hemisphere. The left hemisphere seems to assume a dominant

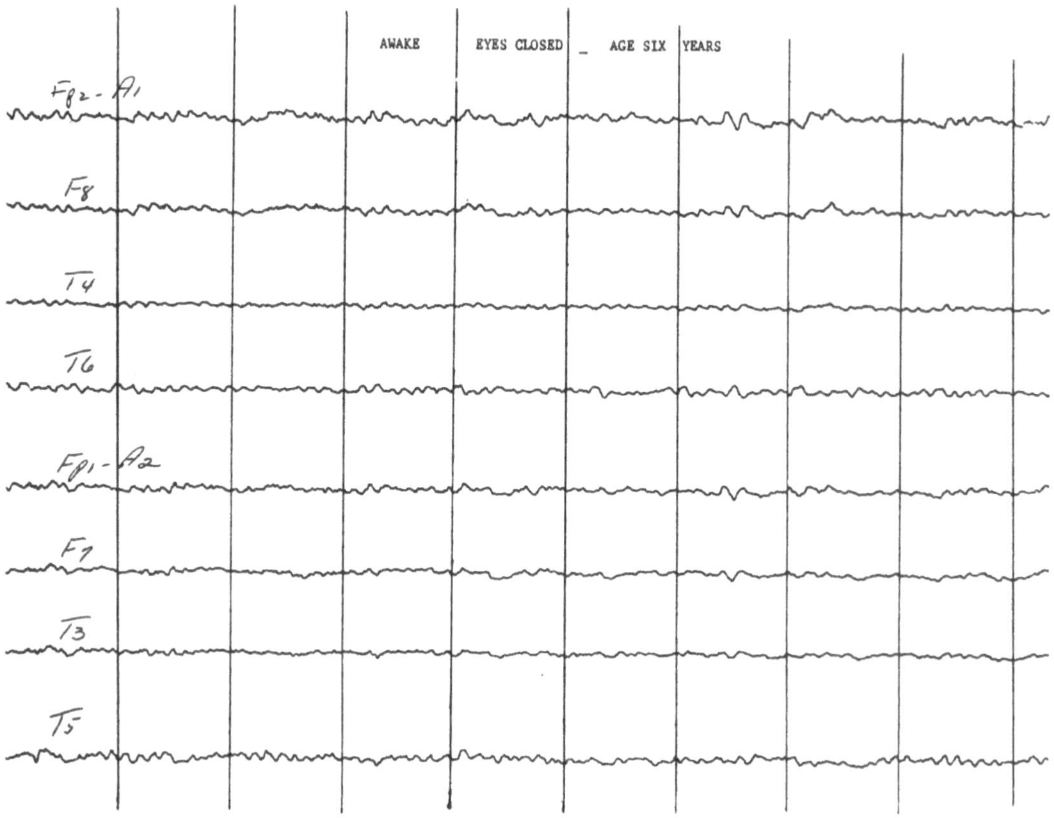

FIGURE 2

Awake and relaxed: normal alpha-type rhythmic activity. Note: the darker vertical lines are at intervals of one second.

role in systematic, analytic, logical, sequential thinking, and in planning. The right hemisphere is more actively involved in a holistic, gestalt, relational, intuitive, synthetic approach to problems. This research may provide a clue to an understanding of differences in abilities, strengths and weaknesses in individuals who may be quite competent in logical, systematic planning but quite unable to make decisions intuitively, or who can achieve an insightful approach to a problem, but cannot plan the actions necessary to carry it through.

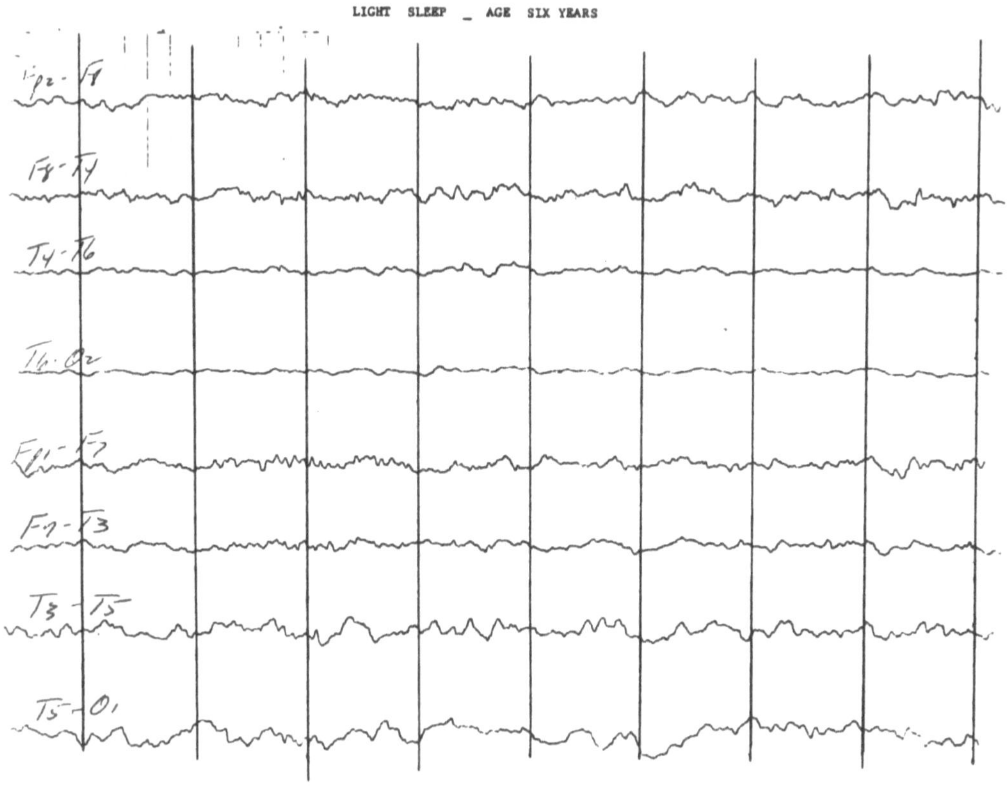

FIGURE 3

Light sleep: decreased frequency, fewer cycles per second; some increase in amplitude.

FIGURE 4

Deep sleep: further decrease in frequency with marked increase in amplitude. As the child falls into deeper sleep, there is an inverse correlation between amplitude and frequency.

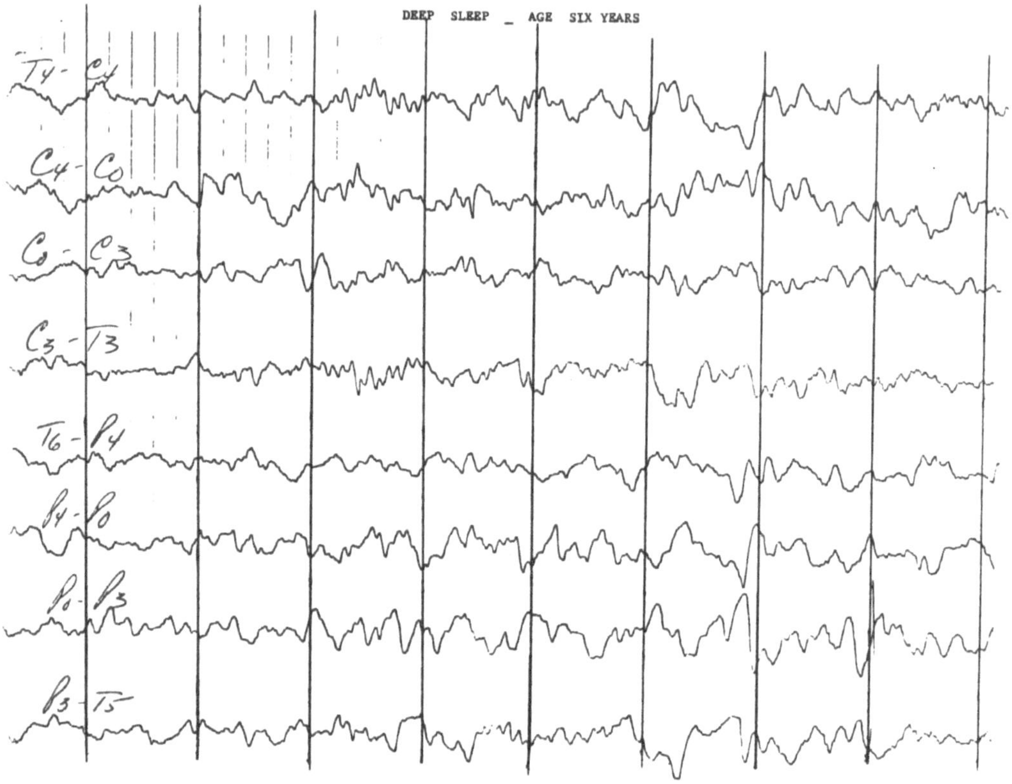

The child's developing brain is practically equipotential in the sense that firm localization of function has not been established in other than the visual cortex in the occipital lobe and in contra-lateral control of movement; consequently, damage to one side of the brain may not have the same permanently disabling effects as in later life.

The patterns of thought present in both hemispheres—intuition and logical analysis—are essential in the acquistion of knowledge. Both right and left hemispheric activities are absolutely necessary, though individuals vary in the degree to which one process may be dominant.

I am tempted to relate all this to the different approach by two of the greatest contributors to our knowledge of child development. I see in Sigmund Freud the characteristics of right-hemispheric thinking: intuition, holistic approach, synthesis, judgment, speculation. In Jean Piaget, I see the characteristics of left hemispheric thinking: systematic, logical, analytical, intellectual approach based on hard data. The aspects of psychology that concerned these investigators determined, to a large extent, the process. Freud's area was man's emotional development, an area enveloped in the darkness of the unconscious, bordering on the esoteric and the mystic, penetrable to intuition and meditation. Piaget's concern has been with cognitive development and with its behavioral and verbal expressions, which are there for all to see in the candid light of day, and which are, therefore, accessible to fact-finding and analysis.

The critical period for brain development

The effects of early malnutrition on structure and function of the central nervous system, and particularly the brain, have been studied experimentally in animals. "The timing of nutritional insufficiency seems to be a critical factor in determining the degree of impairment, its effects being more pronounced when deprivation occurs during the period of most active growth of the brain, that is, during prenatal development" (Di Leo, 1974).

Winick (1968) found a reduction in number of brain cells in rats nutritionally deprived during the first three postnatal weeks. By measuring the total amount of deoxyribonucleic acid in the brain, Winick could conclude that the number of brain cells had been correspondingly reduced.

Studies of children born to nutritionally deprived mothers show reduction in various parameters of growth as well as delay in the attainment of developmental milestones as measured by the Gesell Developmental Schedules. In children who died of marasmus (a pronounced degree of emaciation) before the age of one year, Winick found marked reduction of DNA in their brains, indicating fewer brain cells. Studies of children in deprived populations are in course and, though the evidence is still inconclusive due to concomitant adverse factors (disease, neglect), the deleterious effect of malnutrition before birth and in early infancy is becoming an established fact.

Timing is a crucial factor in the success or failure of the low phenylalanine diet in phenylketonuria (PKU), a recessively inherited metabolic disorder that may result in severe mental retardation if untreated. In affected children who are diagnosed soon after birth and in whom dietary regime is instituted promptly, mental development is safeguarded. In contrast, those children who were untreated until retardation became manifest did not respond significantly to the dietary reduction of phenylalanine, indicating that the retardation had become irreversible.

High priority should be accorded to programs aimed at eliminating malnutrition at all levels but especially during pregnancy and infancy. Preparation for eventual motherhood should begin early in childhood and adolescence to ensure optimum growth and health for future generations.

4

MOTOR DEVELOPMENT

The term "gross motor development" will be used to indicate patterns of posture and locomotion. "Fine motor" will refer primarily to movements of prehension.

The normative sequences have been identified and described by A. Gesell and associates of the Yale Clinic of Child Development.

At birth "the newborn's repertory is replete with a variety of inherited patterned movements, some of them quite striking in their similarity to adaptive responses but for the fact that they express the intelligence of the species and not of the individual. The Darwinian or automatic hand grasp protects the newborn against falling when he is suspended in space, the Moro reflex in response to jarring or loss of support, the toe grasp, the rooting reflex and sucking reflex, the reflex crying are all motor responses to internal or external stimuli, indiscriminate and blind responses but strangely appropriate and oriented towards survival" (Di Leo, 1967).

The asymmetric tonic-neck reflex which dominates posture during the first three months gradually gives way to symmetrical postures of head, trunk and limbs. Rolling over from supine to prone is usually the first volitionally executed change of position. Sitting steadily so that the hands are free to manipulate is achieved by nine months. Creeping and pulling to a standing position soon follow. The first unsteady steps are taken at about a year. By 18 months walking is steady and rapid, while running and climbing impart a sense of individuality. Behavior becomes increasingly assertive as the child is able to walk up and down stairs, jump, ride a tricycle and gradually achieve mastery over the large muscles involved in locomotion.

At the same time, fine motor movements are coming under progressive control. The small eye muscles, having achieved synchronous movement, permit fixation as the child "grasps" with eyes before being able to grasp with hands.

By five months, both hands will reach out and secure a rattle, which will be transferred back and forth from hand to hand in another month. A striking uniquely human accomplishment will occur at about 10 months: the ability to pluck a string between thumb and index finger. This pattern will be further refined during the next few months so that precise pincer grasp will be available during the early part of the second year.

By age three, most children have achieved sufficient mastery over all natural movements (running, climbing, jumping) to permit concentration on purpose or goal without attending to the movements themselves.

Hopping, skipping, broad jump, skating, bicycle riding, dancing, and other gross and fine motor skills can be developed on the basis of the universal postural and motor patterns common to our species. Bipedal locomotion is coded in the DNA of the fertilized ovum.

Development of fine and gross motor behavior

The sequences in gross motor development as described by Gesell and co-workers are in substantial agreement with those of other observers (Pikler, Illingworth, Di Leo) with some variations in the average age given for each sequence:

turns from supine to prone	24 weeks
sits leaning forward on hands for support	28 weeks
sits steadily without support	40 weeks
crawls (drags self forward on belly)	36–40 weeks
creeps (on hands and knees, trunk off surface)	40 weeks
pulls to standing at rail of crib	40 weeks
starts to walk alone	12–15 months
walks well, runs, climbs on chair	18 months

The sequences in fine motor development are as follows:

reflex, automatic hand grasp	0–3 months
ocular fixation and beginning eye-hand coordination	12 weeks
reaching, scratching but unable to secure object	16 weeks
precarious, ulnar-palmar grasp (fifth and fourth fingers press object against palm)	20 weeks
palmar grasp (all four fingers hold object against palm)	24 weeks
radial-palmar grasp (second and third finger hold object against palm)	32–36 weeks
radial raking at a string	32–36 weeks
radial-digital grasp (object secured by thumb, index, and middle fingers)	36–40 weeks
crude release of object	40 weeks
plucks string between index and thumb (pincer grasp)	40–44 weeks
refinement of pincer grasp (neatly plucking from above)	12 months
builds tower of two one-inch cubes	15 months
builds tower of three or four one-inch cubes	18 months

All ages are approximate.

The Gesell norms are based on a study of middle-class New Haven children. It is interesting to note that in a study conducted on 736 normal children reared in the National Methodological Institute for Infant Care in Budapest, Pikler (1968) reported comparable results. The subjects were about evenly divided between males and females. There was no "teaching," that is, other than sufficient space to move about, the infants were kept in supine position until they themselves without assistance were able to roll over, sit, stand, creep, and walk. According to Pikler, not only did the mean age for appearance of the various stages agree with the "best acknowledged developmental scales" but her subjects, uninstructed in motor skills, achieved more adroit, harmonious movements than children reared more conventionally.

In her classic study of *Infants Without Families* (1944), Anna Freud reported even better than average gross motor development in children reared in a residential nursery, although disadvantaged in other areas of greater significance than postural and locomotor patterns.

Relationship of fine and gross motor behavior to total personality

Mittelman (1954) regards motility as an urge or drive in its own right, not merely a component of the other drives (sexual and self-preservation instincts). Though intimately connected with the other urges, motility has its own patterning and organ investment, while its form of expression is dependent upon maturational and cultural influences. Motility of itself is a source of pleasure and satisfaction.

For a prolonged period during 1954, the present writer had the pleasure of having Bela Mittelman as a regular visitor to the Developmental Clinic at New York Foundling Hospital. Observations were made jointly on scores of institution infants brought to the clinic by staff nurses for developmental evaluation. Mittelman's study of motility provided what this writer considers to be the most meaningful insights into the significance of movement.

During the course of the first two years, the earliest, diffuse random movements of the neonate become specifically patterned to accompany a variety of emotional reactions while retaining the rhythmic, auto-erotic rocking and bouncing movements that will eventually recede only to be reactivated in regressive behavior, sexual activity, and other affective-motor behavior.

During the third year, the motor urge (drive) is intense and skilled movements and pleasure in motility reinforce each other as the cortex establishes mastery over the action system.

Movement: Increased and diminished

Intensification of activity may be observed even in the newborn in reaction to restraint, especially when the head is held. Diminution of activity may be seen as early as the first month in some infants as they attend to non-startling visual or auditory stimuli, while more sudden, intense stimuli will provoke a startle (Moro) reflex. Joyous excitement in response to social stimulation is manifested by rhythmic activity of arms and legs in the young infant.

Reactions to strangers and new events become evident after the first six months. The infant is now discriminating strangers and, in the absence of a reassuring mothering figure, the infant will show diminution of activity. In the presence of the maternal object, the infant's hesitation will soon be overcome after turning to look at the mother on whose lap he is sitting. But in the absence of such a known objectified person, he will probably "freeze." Presented with an attractive object, his hand will go out but stop midway, blocked and frozen by conflicting drives. He may remain in this stance of "animated suspension" for prolonged periods, the only movement being that of his roving eyes, alert to the dangers from an unfamiliar situation, while having to rely on his own weak, unsupported ego. Diminution of movement and apathy are likely to be seen in abandoned, depressed infants (anaclitic depression of Spitz).

Persistent rhythmic, non-adaptive activity (rocking, headbanging) are observed in bored, institutionalized infants. This auto-erotic activity was observed to diminish sharply when more and better personal attention was offered and satisfaction began to be derived from the personal and physical environment (Alpert, 1965).

Motility and the body image

The body image results from the confluence of innumerable sensory and motor experiences and, as P. Schilder has noted (1950), it parallels the child's sensori-motor development. The ability to differentiate between self and objects in the environment is closely related to motility. One of the most notable of the infant's achievements is the ability to coordinate eye and hand:

Vision, movements of eye muscles and hands, touch, and kinesthesia are intimately interwoven. With adequate locomotion, the child is able to reach what he sees, to touch and manipulate objects, thus adding another dimension that by integrating the sensory modalities elevates sensation to the level of perception and cognition. "Thus motility becomes one of the most important aspects of reality testing" (Mittelman, 1954).

The increase in motor abilities during the second and third years is associated with assertiveness and self-esteem. The child values his body for what it can do. As cortical control proceeds down the trunk and out into the limbs, movement obeys the eye with increasing fidelity, and the awkwardness of immaturity is replaced by refinement of movement and precision. The child under three delights in the movement that leaves its marks on paper as he scribbles kinesthetically, avidly, and joyously. Past three, he will derive pleasure from his attempts to represent the body image that is maturing in his mind. The human figure is the universally favorite topic of young children past, present, and everywhere. In representational drawing, sense and motion have been elevated to idea and motion. In representational drawing the child is "externalizing a previously internalized mental image" (Piaget and Inhelder, 1971).

To the three-year-old, mastery over movement is an overriding task. The motor urge is intense. Motility, whether in the direction of attack or escape, assumes prominence as a means of self-preservation. Poor motor performance is damaging to the self-image, especially when it draws unfavorable attention from peers who have no hesitation in excluding the awkward one from their games. Derogatory remarks directed at the child by parents who are disappointed at the lack of motor skill can only generate feelings of inferiority and rejection.

The relationship between motility and personality is multifaceted and pervasive.

The sequences in motor development are remarkably uniform. Individual differences are more in the time of emergence of the motor patterns than in the order in which they follow one another.

Attempts to accelerate the developmental tempo have had little effect on those movements that are common endowment of the human species (creeping, standing, walking, grasp) or on the time of extinction of phylogenetic patterns (Moro reflex, automatic hand and toe grasp, tonic-neck reflex, indiscriminate sucking).

Sequences in the development of fine motor control are seen in children's progressive ability to handle crayon and pencil (**Figures 5, 6, 7, 8, 9, 10**). Stage 1—crayon held in fist and brought to mouth; no scribble. Stage 2—crayon held in fist and zig-zag scribble. Stage 3—crayon held in fist but guided by index finger. Stage 4—crayon held between the three radial fingers (thumb, index, middle). Stage 5—crayon or pencil controlled by action of thumb and index and held near point. The ages given are those of the children pictured. The ages at which stages are reached are variable.

The sequences in the development of prehension are described in Gesell and Amatruda's *Developmental Diagnosis*. The maturation of prehension as manifested in drawing with crayon and pencil is described in detail by Rosenbloom and Horton (1971).

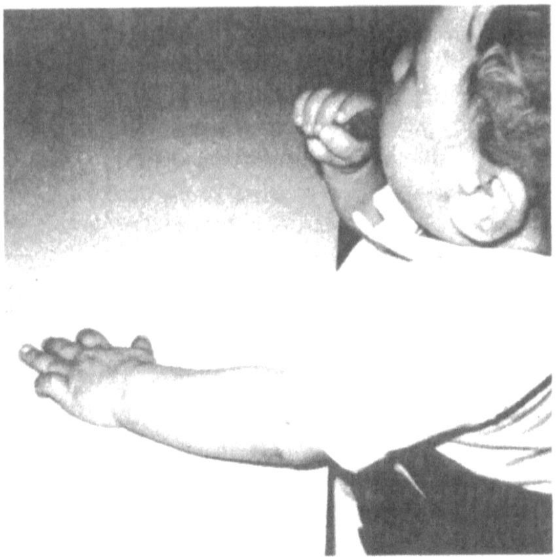

FIGURE 5

Stage 1—crayon held in fist and brought to mouth; no scribble. Age—33 weeks.

FIGURE 6

Stage 2—crayon held in fist and zig-zag scribble. Age—20 months.

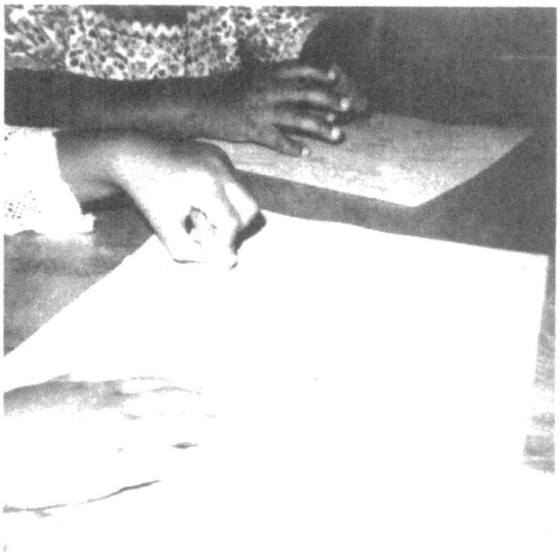

FIGURE 7

Stage 3—crayon held in fist but guided by index finger. Age—24 months.

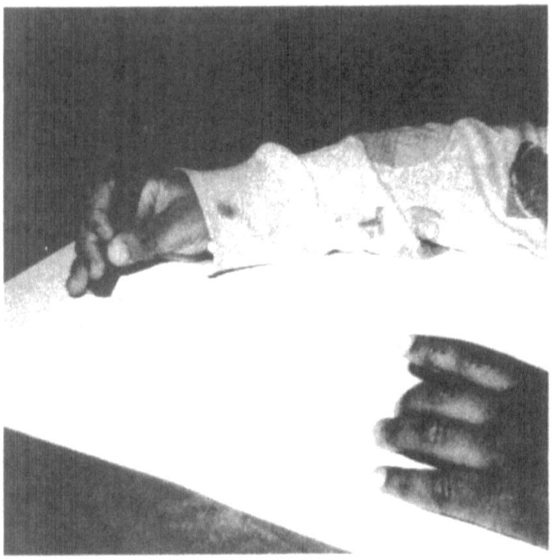

FIGURE 8

Stage 4—crayon is held by the 3 radial fingers: thumb, index, and middle fingers. Age—26 months.

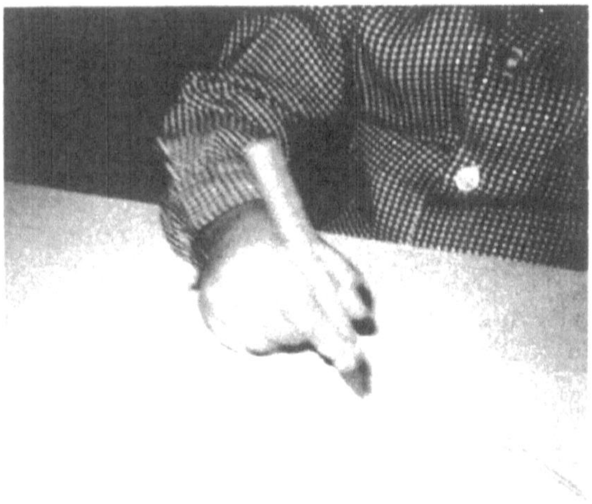

FIGURE 9

Stage 5—crayon or pencil controlled by action of thumb and index and held near point. Age—54 months.

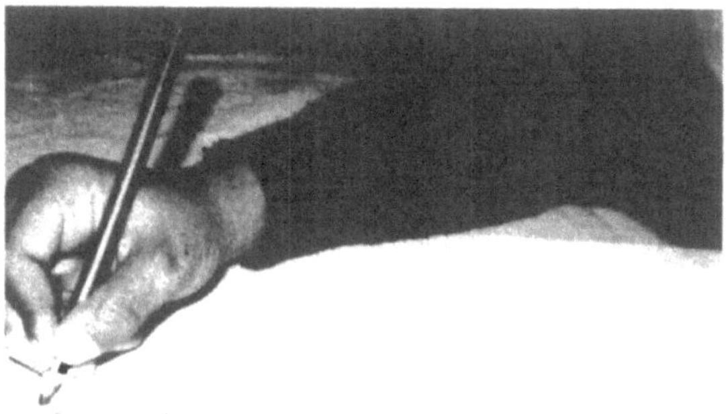

FIGURE 10

Mature action—pencil held near its point; focus of movement in index finger. Age 7.

Some years ago, one of my assistants, who became quite familiar with developmental patterns, brought her own infant of six months for developmental evaluation. She was disappointed when the infant could not do better than was expected of infants his age in attempting to pluck an 8-millimeter pellet. She confessed that she had been training him the past month to do that very thing.

Training is indispensable for the acquisition of skills such as dancing, skating, cycling. It is highly questionable whether there is any wisdom in attempting to accelerate those activities where readiness to perform is intimately related to underlying neural maturation.

5

PSYCHOSEXUAL AND PSYCHOSOCIAL DEVELOPMENT

The stages in psychosexual development

In his theory of infantile sexuality, Sigmund Freud identified a succession of stages in which specific zones of the body provide gratification by being successively endowed with libido, a pleasure-seeking energy. In normative development, the sequences are invariant as one stage is incorporated into the succeeding one that then assumes a dominant role, so that all stages coexist when the individual attains the end-point: mature adult genitality. Arrest or regression to pre-genital levels accounts for neurotic behavior. Progress is marked by gradual transfer of libido to other body zones.

Oral

First is the oral stage during which the libido energizes the mouth. Incorporation is the dominant mode. Gratification is experienced through sucking and then through biting. Mutual pleasure in provider and child makes for a satisfying interaction. The satisfaction of oral needs during this first stage is closely tied to the attainment of a sense of trust. "Taking-in" is the dominant mode during this period, which extends throughout the first year. During this stage the infant treats the mother's body as though it were his own, playing with her hair and features, and even feeding her.

Anal

As oral activity is integrated into the next stage, it surrenders its dominant role to the anal zone. This becomes the field for two conflicting modes: retention or release; yes or no. During this stage of contradictory tendencies, the child is developing a sense of autonomy, which finds expression in physical as well as verbal bravado. The mother definitely becomes part of the outside world. The child runs from her and feels independent, uses the personal pronouns I, me, and mine, and even dares to assert his individuality with a defiant shaking of the head in the ubiquitous semantic gesture and the verbal expression peculiar to his native tongue. This occurs typically during the early part of the second year and marks the beginning of distance communication, as well as the concept and feeling of differentiation from the libidinal object.

The loving, informed parent will regard the child's *no* as an admirable striving towards independence, as a sign of progress and growth. Too often, however, the behavior is misinterpreted as the root and harbinger of a stubborn, willful, uncooperative personality. In most Western cultures, this is considered the time for the acquisition of bladder and bowel control, in utter disregard of the fact that concepts of orderliness and cleanliness are alien to the child's natural inclinations at this time. The premature imposition of adult standards accounts for much compulsive-neurotic behavior in later life. Instead of learning how and why and where to hold on and let go, children will learn instead how to use the power to express rebellion by refusing to comply with that and other demands of the culture. Where the caretakers are loving and aware of the significance of the child's behavior, they will understand that the child of two and three needs time to select between alternatives, that decision and judgment are in their nascent stage, and that the ego is tentatively exercising its function as mediator between the internal world and the outside.

Phallic

Beginning at three and extending through the next three or four years, the child achieves mastery over the action system, as gross and fine motor activity come under efficient control. This stage is also designated as locomotor-genital. Aware of his or her own sex, the child displays curiosity about the mysterious belly-button and about the sex organs of others. Sensual feelings for the parent of the other sex tend to cause feelings of frustration, dissatisfaction with one's own ineffectual sex organs, and hostility toward the powerful rival. This reincarnation of Oedipus and Electra may result in behavior that must be tolerated, understood, and viewed with amusement lest, by severe disapproval, the parent implant the destructive weed of guilt. Progress is made as the child's unsatisfiable feelings are temporarily set aside for substitute gratification in relationships with peers, and in social and physical outlets.

Latency

The next normative sequence is one of *relative* calm beginning with the entry into school and lasting until the dramatic changes of puberty demand a reorientation to the phenomena precipitated by a shower of hormones from the pituitary and gonads. Sexual interests remain active though much psychic energy may be diverted to social activities. The libido finds alternate means of exerting its power as the child derives satisfaction in the pursuit of knowledge. Sexual impulses may be relatively dormant but they are by no means extinct. If preceding stages have been favorably resolved and integrated, this period of latency is one of industry and growing self-esteem. Rather than repressed, the libido is diverted by the ego to meet cultural demands, while transfer of energy is also occurring from parents to extra-familial figures. The child who does not acquire a sense of self-confidence and self-esteem during these years is ill-equipped to meet the challenges of adolescence.

Puberty and adolescence

No longer a child, but not yet an adult, with emotional maturation lagging far behind the spurt in physical, sexual, and intellectual development, the adolescent must reorganize the concepts of self and of the world. During this stage satisfaction of needs will be sought from peers rather than from parents. At first adolescents will seek others of the same sex, with boys and girls staying in homogeneous clusters until the need for the other sex becomes a paramount concern. Under favorable conditions at home and beyond, the struggle to achieve an identity that takes place during these years will lead to a favorable outcome. In the sexual sphere, mature adult genitality will find its eventual fulfillment in a love relationship between a woman and a man.

The stages in psychosocial development

Erik H. Erikson (1950) has provided what is probably the most meaningful blueprint of the stages through which one travels from the helplessness of birth to the ego integrity of the mature adult. Within a psychoanalytic framework, Erikson has emphasized the significance of social development as well as genitality, finding that this latter aspect has often been overemphasized. Erikson has distinguished eight stages in the life cycle from birth to maturity. The scope of this discussion will be limited to the first five stages. As is the case with other stage-dependent theories, the chronological ages are approximate and subject to individual variation, but the sequences are considered to be invariant.

Basic trust

A favorable outcome of development during the first year is basic trust, the child having "learned to rely on the sameness and continuity of the outer providers, . . ." Where maternal care has been defective or lacking, as in congregate shelters, basic mistrust expresses the failure of the ego to resolve its first task.

Autonomy

Depending on this first outcome, the child may or may not enjoy a sense of autonomy during the second and third years. If encouraged to proclaim his individuality within a limiting frame that protects but does not suppress, the outcome will be favorable. Otherwise, a sense of shame and doubt will accompany him through the next cycle.

Initiative

Under favorable conditions of affection and informed guidance of the burgeoning personality, the years from three to six are a time for initiative, experimentation, creativity. Disapproval, criticism, and imposition of adult standards tend to foster a sense of guilt.

Industry

Again, depending on the outcome of previous stages, the child now at school may or may not find satisfaction in scholastic activities and in the company of his peers. If well prepared for these new experiences, the child will apply himself with pleasure, free from crippling anxieties. Away from the family, there is danger of being cruelly subjected to discriminatory practices. A favorable outcome during these years is a sense of industry and satisfaction in acquiring the basic education that is indispensable for progress in society. An unfavorable outcome of these years is a feeling of inadequacy, of inferiority, a lack of self-esteem that weakens motivation and depresses the intellect.

Identity

Youth begins with the advent of puberty and the establishment of a good initial relationship to the world of skills and tools. Biologic and physiologic changes alter the body image and require new adaptations. Emotional ties gravitate from parents to peers, and eventually there comes a need for the opposite sex. The central problems revolve around the acceptance of self, successful interpersonal relationships, and success in preparation for a career. The favorable outcome is identity formation; unfavorable result is identity foreclosure and role confusion.

Within this frame, there is recognition of the need for a loved partner with whom one experiences mutual sexual pleasure as well as mutual trust and respect, and "with whom one is able and willing to regulate the cycles of

a. work
b. procreation
c. recreation . . ." (Erikson, 1950).

Critical period for sex-role orientation in father-absent boys

Numerous studies indicate that timing and duration of the father's absence, as well as failure to provide a father surrogate during the preschool years, adversely affect the boy's assumption of the male sex role.

In their interests, choice of playmates and games, interpersonal relationships, and in tests (It Scale for Children), father-absent boys revealed preference for roles traditionally associated with femininity.

This disparity between biological sex and sex role is also manifested in human figure drawings. The vast majority of young and school-age children will draw their own sex first when asked to draw a person. Fatherless children (and those whose fathers are present in the home but ineffectual, weak, and unattractive because of their punitive attitude) will draw a female figure instead (Di Leo, 1973, p.62).

Money (1965), after investigating the matter, has arrived at the striking conclusion that sex role is established by age three and that it is firmly resistant to change after that time.

The effects of father absence on girls have also been studied but they are not clear. In any case, it does not seem to have as decided an effect on the sex-role orientation of girls as of boys.

The important implication from what has been observed is that attractive parental models of both sexes should be available to the child for sex-role orientation during the preschool years, and, particularly, during the first three years, as that seems to be the critical time.

6

COGNITIVE DEVELOPMENT

The stages in cognitive development

This is a schematic review of Piaget's stage-dependent theory. The present writer is fully aware of the inadequacy of this condensation. It may serve, nevertheless, as an outline for correlation with other stage-dependent theories and, possibly, to support this writer's belief in the interdependence of the complex and diverse elements that go to make up the whole. Piaget's system is selected as offering a most meaningful epistemological discourse on cognitive development.

According to Piaget, the child, in growing from a reflexive to a reflective organism, passes through an invariant sequence of stages that are clearly identifiable within a matrix of continuity.

Sensori-motor

The origins of intelligence are to be found in the inherited capacity to respond reflexly to the stimulus field. Patterned reflexes, present at birth and even before, constitute the organism's first responses to tactile, auditory and other stimuli. Responses which are at first generalized and non-specific become increasingly particular and adaptive with maturation of the underlying neurological substrate. This first period lasts about two years. Piaget calls it *sensori-motor* intelligence. The child thinks motorically. During this basic period outstanding achievements are eye-hand coordination, object permanence (the concept that objects exist even when they cannot be seen or heard), and the ability to use words and their combinations to express needs and wants and feelings. Along with the development of speech is the ability to move away on one's own. As the child achieves bipedal locomotion, there comes an awareness of the self as a separate and distinct entity, an awareness that is given verbal expression in the use of the assertive "I," often emphatically elaborated as "I won't!" At this point problems will be solved by trial and error, not mentally, but the acquirement of the use of words as symbols is a major step in advance towards the next level: the stage of preoperational thought.

Preoperational

During the *preoperational period,* which extends from about two to seven or eight years, impressive gains are made in the use of language. Language, in turn, exerts an increasingly dominant role in the achievement of concepts, particularly in the ordering and classification of the multitude of sensory phenomena that are the child's world. But this is a gradual process extending over five or six years. Things are taken at face value. The world is viewed subjectively. Time is now or near now. Space is the distance from me but near me. The moon follows me as I walk. Imagination and fantasy are ripe as improbable causes are invoked to account for effects. Everything can be accounted for. The child is learning to count and eventually (usually by age $4^1/_2$) can tell the sum—an abstraction. The child is egocentric but, as the end of this period approaches, the child may begin to take the view of other people, though still unable to tell the right and left hand of the person facing. Human figure drawings express the child's subjective view with total disregard of actual body proportions. Instead there is an emphasis on what is regarded as important—intellectual not visual realism. Dominated by his perceptions, the child believes that the quantity of water is greater when poured into a tall glass than when in a wider, shorter one.

Concrete operations

At about the age of seven or eight, most children reach the next level: *the stage of concrete operations.* A notable achievement during this period of intense intellectual growth is the ability to organize material on a higher, more general level. An orange is no longer "something you eat"—it is a fruit; a bicycle will eventually become more than "something with two wheels" as it becomes "something you ride" and then "a vehicle." The child is now able to reverse. In mathematics he can multiply as well as divide. He can tell which is the right and left hand of the person sitting opposite; earlier, he pointed to the mirror image of his own hand. Less egocentric, he is beginning to see and feel how things are experienced by others. As intellectual realism gives way to visual realism, the child's increasing objectivity is reflected in the more realistic proportions of his human figure drawings.

In a series of original experiments, Piaget has shown how the child acquires concepts of conservation and how these concepts are acquired in an invariant order. Conservation of quantity, weight, and volume is understood in that sequence. No longer dominated by his perceptions, the child maintains the concept of conservation despite irrelevant changes in the stimulus field. Concept now dominates perception. By assimilation of the knowledge acquired by acting upon the sensory material, and by accommodation to a novel situation, the child, equipped with concepts of conservation and with the ability to categorize by conceptual instead of perceptual factors, is now ready to function at the next level of intellectual development: the stage of formal operations.

FIGURE 11

In this drawing by a boy of 8½ years, the lower part of the trunk and the legs are seen through the skirt. Transparencies (X-ray technique) indicate that he is still functioning at a preoperational level (Piaget) and that his drawing is still within the stage of "intellectual realism" (Luquet). He draws what he knows to exist, regardless of whether it can actually be seen. He attends an ungraded class. The delay in mental development is reflected in his drawing.

Formal operations

Formal operations are characterized by abstract thinking and logical reasoning. The child is able to consider hypotheses and ignore content as he becomes less dependent on information in the immediate stimulus field. Capable of inductive as well as deductive reasoning, he is able to test a hypothesis, draw logical conclusions, and consider more than one variable. During the earlier stage, the child could classify large and small apples but not large green and small red, when small green and large red had to be eliminated from the grouping.

The level of formal operations may be regarded as the final stage in intellectual functioning. It begins gradually, at some time between eleven and fifteen years, and stays with us until senility and infirmity rob us of this uniquely human function.

With the development of the critical sense at this time, children may lose interest in the visual arts or in music if dissatisfied with their productions. They may then turn to activities that are more appropriate for self-expression and better suited to their abilities.

7

LANGUAGE DEVELOPMENT

infant (in'fant),n. (Latin, *infans*, *-ntis*, unable to speak. *in*, not +*fans*, pres.p. of *fari*, to speak).

A basic element in Piaget's theory is the view that action comes before conceptualization and that there is a logic of action prior to and independent of the development of expressive language. During the first two years, indiscriminate reflex responses evolve into logical actions. The child is still practically nonverbal. His thought can be seen in his adaptive responses; his inner language is evident to the observer. The child learns meanings long before he learns words.

After two, the role of the spoken language becomes increasingly pervasive as the child passes from the stage of sensorimotor intelligence to the preoperational stage and the beginning of symbolic thought.

The stages in language development

Language comprises all forms of communication: crying, facial expression, gesture, touching, yelling, and also speech and writing. These last two are the most highly developed symbolic media for the transmission of culture. Speech is the most efficient form of immediate, interpersonal exchange among humans. Its development is dependent upon the ability to hear and understand, but more especially upon the prior establishment of other more primitive forms of interaction between infant and provider.

More than any other aspect of development, language is influenced by the environment. Although it too follows a sequential, orderly progression, the identification of stages beyond infancy is rendered difficult because of the decisive role of the child's interpersonal relationships and the verbal input. The language spoken is modeled upon the language heard.

Despite the difficulty in setting norms, there are broad sequences that are universal and invariant. These have been identified by Myklebust (1954) as: inner language, receptive language, and, finally, expressive language. Again, the age at which each stage is reached is variable but the order is not. The child is able to think and act meaningfully long before acquiring the words that symbolize objects and actions. With the development of expressive language, the reciprocal interaction of thought and symbols enhances both. Within this broad framework, it may be said that the hearing child, who is not emotionally disturbed, mentally retarded, asphasic, brain-damaged, or environmentally deprived, will smile to his mother at about six weeks, start making vowel sounds by eight weeks, add consonants at about six months, lallate da-da or its equivalent at nine months, say a word or two at one year, start jargon soon after, have a vocabulary of about 10 words at 18 months, and then acquire expressive language at an impressive rate so that by age two, the words used may be over two hundred; but even more striking is the child's use of sentences of three words in which the personal pronouns "I' and "me" are distinctive features, expressing individuality and assertiveness. From then on, vocabulary increases rapidly and innumerable words are available for arrangement in syntactical patterns peculiar to the native tongue.

The potential for speech—but not for any particular form of speech—is inherited. There is no special inborn affinity for the mother tongue; that must be acquired just as any other. Such a notion is suggested by the difficulty encountered by some ethnic groups in pronouncing the sounds of other languages, as in the case of many French-speaking individuals who have a problem with the English "th" sound.

All humans develop speech in basically the same progressions. The first utterances of the neonate are primarily motor, part of the generalized activity that is unrelated to any specific stimulus, automatic, and apparently meaningless.

Within a month or two, the sounds become more differentiated and detectably in response to stimuli from the outside. The sensori-motor components of the reflex arc are now clear as the movement and sound produced occur in response to touch, light, or sound, as well as to stimuli from within. At this time, many mothers claim that the sounds produced by the infant can tell them whether they express a need for food, change of clothing, or body contact.

As the cortex extends its control down the neural axis, babbling and lallation become expressions of volition. Imitation and identification lead to the acquisition of jargon and words. These are at first linked to objects and actions. Eventually, they become the adequate media for the expression of ideas.

In the process of learning language, hearing, comprehension, ability to decode what is heard and to encode in order to express, are all indispensable components of the sensori-neuromuscular mechanism at the service of man's highest psychic functions.

The remarkable capacity of children all over the world to acquire the language of their culture, regardless of its structure and complexity, has been a most fascinating subject for study, investigation, and speculation.

Research continues in the hope of shedding more light upon this universal phenomenon. In its essence, it still remains a field for psychological theory and philosophical speculation.

A good deal is known about the sequences through which the reflex cry of birth becomes the symbolic vehicle for the transmission of ideas. More is being learned of the underlying neurologic structures and functions that make possible the decoding and encoding of the spoken and written word. Intrinsic and environmental influences that favor or impede language acquisition have been identified. But beyond that, the field is obscure.

The universality of the young child's capacity to master the native tongue, regardless of its surface linguistic structure, suggests the existence of an innate capacity to acquire the deeper structures of language. Speculation as to the nature of this innate capacity has divided theorists into two major groups. One, behavioristic in its approach, ascribes the dominant role to input, granting to what is innate simply a selective receptor function and a mechanism for processing. The other view, affirmed by Chomsky, is related to the theory of innate ideas developed by Descartes. Chomsky (1964–66) holds that experience elicits, but does not form, the innate structures of language. These are universally present and account for the child's capacity to create language, to produce sentences that he has never heard, to acquire and to use not only the surface linguistic structure, but also its semantic intent. The innate factor would be a common denominator; the surface linguistic structure would be the variant.

A major impetus to the study of linguistics has been Chomsky's theory of transformational grammar, in which creativity assumes a central role. Imitation cannot account for the commonly noted fact that children produce sentences that they have never heard. Adult words are used to invent new sentences, creatively rather than imitatively. Brown (1973) has provided remarkable insights into the process. His studies show that what the child acquires are the rules of construction of his native tongue. The acquisition is unconscious. The errors in the child's speech are due to inconsistencies in the mother tongue.* Brown has identified an invariant sequence of stages as sentence length and complexity increase with maturity. The stages can be related to the sequences in cognitive development described by Piaget and appear, indeed, to be the linguistic expression of the various levels of intelligence.

Language development correlated with chronological age and motor development

Lenneberg (1967) has approached the study of language in the context of development biology. Though there is considerable variability in the time element, a remarkable regularity is

*As an example Brown cites the word "hisself" commonly used by children in logical extension of the rule that prevails when my, your, our, and her are combined with self to form the reflexive pronoun. The adult breaks the rule and decrees that "himself" is correct.

evident in the sequences and in their correlation with motor development. Both language and motor development attain their fulfillment at a rate that parallels certain physical parameters of brain development, notably weight and maturation of the cerebral cortex. Lenneberg cautions against interpreting the correlations as proof of causal connections, but the universality and regularity of the sequences, and the parallel attainment of "milestones" in motor and language development are suggestive of the basic unity that embraces all aspects of maturation.

The child's first words are usually heard as he or she begins to walk unaided. Sentence formation accompanies the ability to move about freely, to run, and to walk up and down stairs at age two. Language is well established as the child attains mastery over the action system by age four.

A distinction must be made between the ability to achieve and its realization. Of all aspects of development, language is the most affected by the social, cultural, and affective milieu. Despite the restraints of my scientific background, I will not hesitate to make this general statement: All institutionalized infants and children are delayed in language development. The same applies to those children who exist in a loveless home. This fact has been stressed by Anna Freud and has been unequivocally confirmed by my own long experience.

In one institution, I asked a boy of three, "What is your name?" He pointed to the tape on his wrist. He had plenty of inner language, as well as comprehension, but he was seriously impaired in his ability to verbalize. The impediment was not organic in any way.

There is no doubt that language stimulation is an important element in the development of language. But even more essential is the in-depth, ongoing, affective relationship with parental figures. Speech is useless if there is nothing to tell, nothing to share with someone who really cares.

Critical period in language development

In the mature brain, speech centers are mainly in the left hemisphere in the vast majority of persons, regardless of whether they are right- or left-handed. Damage to the left side of the brain is likely to result in loss of the faculty of speech (aphasia). Such is not the case in young children. The developing brain is equipotential in the sense that localization has not as yet been established. That is why damage to the left side of the developing brain may not result in persistent loss of the power of speech. According to Lenneberg (1969), the early teens may be considered to be the critical period for both acquisition and restoration of speech. It is interesting to note that the adult encephalographic pattern of 9-11 per second alpha rhythm is established at that time.

Learning a language becomes progressively more difficult as the child approaches adolescence. The difficulty is not limited simply to acquiring the proper enunciation; it extends beyond to the grammatical and syntactical structure.

Acquisition of second languages

Children acquire phonemes easily. But more impressive is the ease with which they acquire the language code in its receptive, expressive, and affective as well as cognitive components.

If exposed to good speech models, many bright children are capable of expressing themselves in two and even more languages with remarkable fluency. This ability never fails to astound the adult who is having such a hard time pronouncing his French grammar and garbling the syntax.

Adults who are truly bi- or tri-lingual, having acquired the languages during their early childhood, are well aware that language is not simply a matter of sentences, grammar, and syntax. The shift from one language to another is associated with striking changes in the personality of the speaker. A reserved manner proper to English gives way to a more ebullient attitude reinforced with appropriate facial expressions and gestures when the same person is conversing in Italian.

Returning to the ease with which young children acquire languages, a subject which has fascinated me, I have often wondered why this facility is gradually lost as the child matures. As the child progresses in age and cognition, another language can be acquired only by laborious application to pronunciation, grammar, and syntax. It seems to me that the reason for the progressive decline lies in the shift of focus that occurs in the child's development. From about the age of two, through the preschool years, the drive to verbalize assumes an intensity comparable to that of mastering bipedal locomotion during the earlier years. Talking becomes a major activity. Children talk at another child but not with the other. They are often heard talking to themselves. It is a game played by one person. The point of view of the other is ignored. During these years one can hardly regard talking as a conversation. It is absorbing to the point of being an end in itself. Such intense involvement accounts for the facility in acquiring languages, a facility that declines as the focus shifts to communication and expression of thought. With the gradual decline in egocentricity, there is greater use of language as a means. Speech becomes a tool, no longer the focus, and with this change it enters the areas of cognitive and interpersonal activity to an increasing degree. The one-time facility is gradually lost to a more important function in the hierarchy of human behavior.

8

DRAWING BEHAVIOR

The stages in development of drawing behavior

The stages in maturation of drawing behavior were clearly described and brilliantly interpreted by G. H. Luquet in "Les Dessins d'un Enfant: Étude Psychologique," published in 1913. The author had kept every drawing, a total of 1700, made by his daughter Simonne from age 3.3 to 8.8 years of age. In studying this impressive collection, Luquet was able to identify distinct levels within the continuum. He interpreted these levels or stages as representing expressions of the maturing mind of the child, qualitatively different from that of the adult. The stages have been confirmed by investigators in many lands and diverse cultures, in drawings by children past and present and from a variety of social backgrounds. The interpretation by Luquet remains the basis for an understanding of the drawings as expressions of the child's unique perceptions and concepts.

In common with children everywhere, the favorite model for Simonne's artistic endeavors was the human body. After all, what is more important in a child's life than people!

A major distinctly qualitative division may be made between scribbling and representational drawing.

Kinesthetic

In scribbling or kinesthetic drawing, which begins at about 15 months, the child delights in the movement that leaves its mark. Sense and motion combine as the child enjoys the zig-zag that will gradually evolve through lines and arcs into circles at age three, a prelude to the moment of truth when the discovery is made that the circle produced so casually can be made to represent something in reality, something very much in mind: a human face. The bridge has been crossed although the child may return to former territory for nostalgic comfort in moments of stress.

First symbol

Now the child is able to create a symbol. Chimpanzees can produce kinesthetic art, but only man creates symbols. Representational art is symbolic and distinctly human.

Representation

Luquet's contribution to our understanding begins with the advent of representational drawing. This breakthrough occurs in most children sometime between three and four. The term "creativity" may now be more properly applied to the child's product as the intention to represent guides the uncertain hand that delineates a barely recognizable figure. The product of kinesthetic drawing could be called a creation only in that it was something that had not been there before. That stage has been superseded and forgotten, but not extinguished.

Intellectual realism

In the first phase in representational drawing, the object simply serves as a cue, not as a visual model to be reproduced. The child draws an internal model. If the drawing is of a person, the result will be identical whether the person is actually present or not. If you sit in front of a child under seven, offering a profile view, you will be drawn standing and full-face. Luquet has called this intellectual realism. The drawing will show what is known rather than what can actually be seen. Important features will be emphasized. Perspective will be of a different order than visual; the significant elements will be drawn larger regardless of location; persons in a house will be visible through the walls. The child attempts to show what is known to exist, not just what can actually be seen. Awareness of what is being attempted provides insight into the meaning of peculiarities in child art. The uninformed adult may try to correct the child's direct, fresh view, misinterpreting it as "wrong." The drawings are subjective because the child's thought is subjective. The child draws as he reasons and reasons as he draws.

Visual realism

Luquet has called the next stage visual realism. The child, now about seven, attempts to draw from observation. The drawings reflect to an increasing degree the actual appearance of objects. Transparencies gradually disappear. Men are no longer visible through the hull of a ship. Legs are no longer seen through trousers. The drawings will show an awareness of visual perspective and physical proportions. Heads will no longer dominate bodies by their size. Big will be drawn those persons who are actually big in size rather than in significance. The X-ray see-through technique of the previous stage will give way to a more visually realistic portrayal. At age nine, when most children begin to draw a profile (prelude to drawing the figure in motion), a carry-over from the earlier stage will cause the child to draw a second eye and a second nose; but this "error," too, will give way to visual realism. Probably the most distinctive characteristic of visual realism is the attempt to represent visual perspective. The child is becoming more objective in thought and consequently in graphic activity. This stage continues through the adolescent years and, for most, marks the end-point in drawing ability. Most of us as adults draw no better than when we were ten. With the development of the critical sense, only those who are satisfied with their drawings are likely to seek training to improve skill and aesthetic sensitivity. The majority will turn to other activities for satisfaction.

These stages are united by transitional phases during which there is frequent reversion to earlier patterns of drawing, just as in all other aspects of behavior.

In essence, what is occurring in the development of graphic activity is a gradual passage through successive, invariant sequences from a purely sensori-motor scribbling to the realization that marks can be made to symbolize one's perception and concept of reality; that the figures drawn, at first subjective and unconsciously expressionistic, eventually become more objective and impressionistic—still personal but more influenced by the reality outside one's self—less a statement about the artist than about the object. That is why children's drawings are more revealing of thought and feelings during the preschool and early school years when cultural influences and pressures are more likely to be resisted or ignored.

Arnheim (1954) comments on the influence of the medium on the art of children. Unfamiliarity with the medium impairs and restricts the child's ability to portray all that he perceives, thinks, and feels, even if that were his intention. But, granted the limitations, crayon in the very young, and pencil in those who can manage it, permit greater ease of control and clarity of stroke and detail than other media such as paint or modeling.

As noted by Erikson, the child during the school years may be subjected to cruel discriminatory practices at the hands of his peers, with resultant loss of self-esteem. Dennis (1966) has used human figure drawings by school-age children to evaluate group values on the assumption that school-age children will draw the type of man they admire. In this connection it is interesting to note that black children are increasingly drawing figures with black features (Afro hair-style, prominent lips and nares). This tendency is interpreted as an expression of increasing acceptance and pride in their racial status.

Prior to school age, I have found it impossible to distinguish drawings by white children from those by non-whites. However, the figures drawn do tend to show sex preference and, in a family grouping, the parent or sibling most admired, as indicated by first placement in the group.*

*For a fuller discussion of children's drawings the reader is referred to my two books on the subject, listed in the bibliography (Di Leo, 1970, 1973).

Transition

There is no sharp line of demarcation that separates one stage of development from the next. In progressing towards maturity, each stage evolves imperceptibly into the next, while retaining its own features. Under stress, the individual may seek refuge in an earlier level of adaptation, since it is always available.

But even in the course of normal progression, there are frequent back-slidings. The child is said to take two steps forward and one step backward.

Summary and implications

There is general agreement on the sequences in the development of visual symbolization. The number of sequences may vary if transitional phases are regarded as stages. Luquet considers four "phases" as distinct while recognizing the continuity and transitional nature of graphic development.

1. The first period, generally referred to as kinesthetic or scribbling, is involuntary in that the child is as yet unaware that the configurations can represent an object.
2. The breakthrough or discovery must have been a thrilling moment when we first saw something in our casually drawn circular figure. Was it a head into which we then drew two smaller circles, the eyes?
3. Luquet regards the third period the "apogee" in the development of drawing. During this stage, the child is revealing a view of realities that many of us have lost. The fortunate ones have tried to retain its essence or to recapture it. The great Roumanian sculptor, Constantin Brancusi, expressed it visually in "The Kiss" and verbally "quand nous ne sommes plus enfants, nous sommes déja morts." The child's drawings during this period express a fresh, direct, subjective concept of the world of persons and things. The adult is ill-advised to rush the child out of this delightful stage, to "educate" the child out of it. Left to themselves and the maturing influence of growth, children will gradually pass into the next stage without need for adult direction.

4. "Réalisme visuelle." By degrees, and hopefully without interference, the child will attempt to depict objects more as the outer eye sees them. This stage is an advance only if creativity and originality have not been sacrificed on the altar of conformity to an alien view. Art education at this stage may do more harm than good when it does not take into account the child's need to think and act as an individual within a tolerant culture. Drawings will now show an awareness of visual perspective and actual body proportions. Many adults will be pleased with these changes but the child will have lost something. The imposition of "correct" standards may cause the child to lose it all.

Chronological age is but an approximate norm for the time when the various stages prevail. Developmental age is a better guide. In normal children, sequences are invariant and there is a positive correlation with cognitive development. Pressure and practice may seem to accelerate the process, but the concept will not really be possessed until earlier levels have been reached and assimilated. And it is better for all this to happen in the individual child's own good time.

9

DEVELOPMENTAL ARREST

Biological

In physical maturation and particularly in organogenesis, toxins, viruses, and radiation are well known causes of arrested growth and development of organs and parts of the body. Cardiac malformations, rudimentary limbs, and microcephaly are striking examples of such arrest.

Psychosexual

In Freudian theory of psychosexual development, neurotic afflictions are often attributed to fixation at intermediate stages blocking progress towards mature genital sexuality. Fixation may occur at any of the pregenital levels so that gratification may be sought from stimulation of early erogenous zones (oral, anal), or from other auto-erotic or "immature" sexual activity, finding expression at times in sadistic, masochistic, or hysterical behavior, at times in sublimation and, perhaps, in impressive artistic performance.

Severe forms of developmental arrest are seen in young psychotic children. In the autistic group, one can hardly speak of arrest since there has not even been a beginning of attachment to the mothering person; living and inanimate objects are treated alike. In the symbiotic group, there is true developmental arrest. In these children, the normal early symbiotic relationship with the caretaker has been established but there is no progress beyond this stage to the object-libidinal cathexis of the mother. These children strive to perpetuate the "delusional omnipotence phase of the mother-infant fusion of earliest times . . ." (Mahler, 1952).

Psychosocial

In his stage-dependent theory of psychosocial development, Erikson emphasizes the early relationship between infant and caretaker as the foundation for subsequent mental health. This early task of the ego has been achieved when the infant by the end of the first year has developed firm positive feelings toward the most important person in his young life, feelings that Erikson calls a sense of basic trust. Upon this foundation, the ego finds the strength to cope with an expanding personal environment, and to grow from a sense of autonomy, initiative, industry, and identity to reach an ego integrity that can stand up to powerful adverse cultural pressures.

A weak foundation during the child's infancy will cause the superstructure of the personality to be less stable, less capable of successfully confronting the problems inherent in growing up. Psychic energy then tends to be trapped at intermediate stages resulting in feelings of shame, guilt, worthlessness, and lack of motivation. Hopelessness and frustration during adolescence can block the need to accept one's self and to progress toward satisfying experiences in love and work. Arrest of psychosocial development during this period because of devaluation and depreciation of self results in identity foreclosure, the young person settling for a minor role. It is important to keep in mind that the forces operating for better or worse are not just intrapsychic but that powerful environmental influences are at play. Even with a good beginning, the child may encounter strong, frustrating, negative, discriminatory influences during the school and adolescent years.

Cognitive

According to Piaget, the child's cognitive development occurs in an invariant order through successive stages or levels of intellectual maturity. This is a stage-dependent theory similar to a mathematical model so that progress depends upon the assimilation and integration of each preceding stage. Accordingly, failure to progress beyond a given stage implies delayed intellectual development which, depending on its nature, may or may not respond to habilitative measures. A profoundly retarded child may never progress beyond the sensori-motor level. A moderately retarded one may function at the level of concrete operations without ever reaching the level of formal operations. Then there may be a selective developmental halt in which only specific concepts may present difficulty rather than an overall arrest at an immature cognitive stage. Of this type are difficulties limited to the field of mathematical operations or language or perceptual function without across-the-board delayed development. A variety of causes may be responsible for poorly integrated behavior—genetic, emotional, traumatic, cultural—to name a few.

Language

The onset of mutism in a child who had previously been speaking may be indicative of a serious emotional disorder. In her work with psychotic children, Margaret Mahler has described this communication disorder in children who had failed to extricate themselves from the normal symbiotic state that prevails during the first six months and who, when separation became inevitable, reacted to the crisis by becoming mute, often with associated manifestations of hostility directed against self or mother. This symptomatology may burst forth at age three or four or even later and manifests the overwhelming anxiety suffered by the child whose ego development could not free itself from its complete tie to the mother.

Motor

Arrest of motor development is primarily a neurological or orthopedic problem affecting the growing organism. Damage to the brain or spinal cord may prevent a child from ever reaching the stage of bipedal locomotion. Cerebral palsy, cord injury, and cerebellar syndromes are examples.

Drawing

In drawing behavior, developmental arrest can hardly be called a pathological feature since it seems to occur in most of us in the sense that as adults we can draw no better than we could at age ten or so. Talented persons are, of course, exceptions to this generalization.

As noted earlier, decline of interest in drawing is commonly seen in adolescents, who previously may have been drawing avidly. This shift away from drawing is influenced by development of the critical sense at this age. The adolescent now sees the work more objectively and more critically, tends to be dissatisfied, and turns to other more effective and satisfying means for self-expression.

In drawing behavior, developmental arrest is manifested in the discrepancy between the human figure drawing and the norms for the child's chronological age. This statement, while generally valid, requires qualification. Pure body image as reflected in drawings may not be a measure of intellectual capacity in children who are emotionally disturbed, brain-damaged, or impaired in sensory, motor, or perceptual function. Human figure drawings by retarded children not otherwise handicapped are an expression of the intellectual level at which they are functioning at that time. The Goodenough-Harris test is widely used as part of a comprehensive test battery. The notion of arrested development should not be interpreted as proclaiming finality. There is abundant evidence that the IQ is not constant and that dealing with abstract material is not the only form of coping with life in a community. Training and special education have demonstrated their effectiveness in elevating the functional level of many children, who had been tagged with what might have been a permanent label.

10

REGRESSION

Reversion to an earlier level of adaptation may occur in any of the aspects of development.

Psychosexual

In psychosexual development, the child under stress may exhibit behavior of any earlier stage: oral, anal, locomotor-genital. In mental illness, regression may retrace the steps back to the infantile or even intra-uterine period. Schizophrenic patients may assume the fetal posture of flexion as they return to the stage of passivity that prevailed in the womb. Phases of regressive behavior are commonly seen in children who feel threatened by the arrival of a new baby, expressing their anxiety by demanding the breast or bottle and by soiling and wetting though they had already achieved habit training. Preschool children faced with the uncertainties of a visit to the doctor may present with thumb in mouth seeking consolation in an earlier, but still available, level of gratification. Persistent, habitual oral activity—sucking and biting—into the preschool years may be due to oral deprivation during the first year.

Auto-erotic habits, such as rocking, head-banging and finger-sucking, which had been outgrown, may be resumed during illness with consequent restriction of movement. Similar regressive behavior may occur in two-year-olds who have been separated from their mothers.

In therapeutic psychoanalysis, regression through transference is necessary so that conflicts at earlier psychosexual stages may be identified and resolved, and sexual energy disengaged for healthy progression toward maturity.

Psychosocial

Erikson has described psychosocial development as an orderly resolution of tasks that beset the ego in its progression from birth to maturity as it interacts with a widening social field.

In this progression series of challenges are identified as stages. The stages are dependent upon previous stages which have been resolved and incorporated into the maturing personality. As with all other aspects of development, each challenge may be met in full, in part, or not at all, resulting in a personality that is healthy and strong, or vulnerable and weak. In the latter case, stress may occasion a return to earlier, safer ground, to a narrower, more restricted social field. In regression, the movement backwards may be temporary while the ego reorganizes its forces or the danger moves away.

Erikson regards the sense of basic trust that develops during the first year as the cornerstone of a healthy personality. The abiding effects of the infant's earliest encounters with a maternal figure are reflected in the behavior of child and adult. Optimum development is fostered when the interaction between infant and mother evolves in an atmosphere of reciprocal gratification. Unreasonable distrust and withdrawal in later life may have had its origin in a failure to achieve a sense of basic trust during the first year.

Cognitive

Regression to a previously surpassed level of cognitive functioning occurs during transition from stage to stage or while a concept is being acquired. But once the concept is assimilated, consolidated, and accommodated to novel situations, regression does not occur except under pathological conditions or aging. "Once you know, you know for always." While this is generally true, it cannot be interpreted to mean that attaining to a higher cognitive level disposes of the preceding stage. The child may not be functioning at the same conceptual level in all areas. A child of seven who has mastered conservation of quantity will very likely be thinking in pre-operational terms for the next several years before being able to understand the concept of conservation when it applies to weight or volume. But once these concepts have been mastered, the child will regard as foolish the notion that weight is dependent upon volume or that quantity changes with shape.

Language

Regression in language may occur as a manifestation of sibling jealousy in children of three or so who are called upon to welcome a new addition to the family. Among the various ways of expressing concern and the need for reassurance, there may be imitation of the baby's condition that is receiving so much attention: incontinence, demand for breast or bottle, excessive crying, mutism, or baby talk. Older children who have developed interests outside the family are less likely to regard the new arrival as a dangerous usurper and are consequently less likely to imitate his ways.

Symbiotic children who respond to separation from the mother by becoming mute may, when speech returns, recapitulate the earlier sequences. Baby talk and other infantile patterns of speech may reappear before the original level of fluency is regained.

Young children may lose their newly acquired ability to speak as a result of absence of the mother. In describing the effects of evacuation of children, rendered necessary during the air-raids on London, Anna Freud noted the loss of speech among the retrograde phenomena occasioned by separation from the mother. This has also been observed when children are separated from their mothers and placed into shelters, regardless of the reason. Even when the separation is unavoidable because of illness, the loss of contact can never be accepted as necessary or beneficial by the young child, who can only regard the situation as one of abandonment and rejection. Regression in language is only one aspect of the child's hurt. For this and many other reasons, when a child must be hospitalized, particularly between the ages of two and five, the parent should be given sleep-in privileges.

Motor

Reversion to an earlier form of locomotion occurs normally until the more advanced pattern has been established as a part of the regular behavioral repertory. For example, an infant may start walking a few steps at ten months and then go back to creeping for another two months. At times, this relapse to an earlier pattern has been observed in children who had started walking but were hurt or frightened by a fall.

Temporary resumption of crawling and creeping has been seen in children of preschool years in their attempt to gain the attention of parents by imitating the behavior of the new addition to the family.

Among the disorders of motility that may occur in psychotic states are regressions to childhood, infantile, or even intra-uterine levels of posture and locomotion.

Duchenne type of muscular dystrophy may cause a child who had been walking and running freely to gradually retrace the steps of motor development as far back as a state of immobility.

In a series of observations made jointly by Bela Mittelman and Di Leo, a striking reduction of motility was typically seen in depressed infants without families. The group studied were in the second half of the first year and were brought to developmental clinic for evaluation of behavior. They were accompanied by a nurse. Their behavior was in striking contrast to that of secure infants who, accompanied by their mothers, soon felt safe enough to respond by securing the test objects and exploiting them. These infants would often remain motionless for long periods, except for movement of the eyes, as they scanned the environment that seemed to threaten them from all directions. Presented with an attractive object, they would instinctively reach out but "freeze" midway, wanting to take the object but not daring to make this move. They might remain in this "freeze" position for more than five minutes.

Drawing

In the development of drawing, "the passage from stage to stage is never abrupt. It proceeds by degrees, with frequent lapses into earlier levels but with an onward and upward trend into the higher level" (Di Leo, 1970).

A girl of five and a half draws a clearly recognizable female figure. Then, suddenly, overpowered by feelings of hostility apparently directed against the person represented, she reverts to scribbling over the drawn figure. A burst of negative feelings has resulted in reversion to their expression at an earlier, more primitive level of graphic activity.

When drawing a single human body, the child tends to draw a figure that is both quantitatively and qualitatively better than those he draws in a family group. This writer believes the reason for the difference to reside in the attitude of the child. In drawing the single figure, the child is more likely to express what he knows or recalls. In drawing the family, feelings are mobilized, as relationships and status enter the situation. The cognitive-affective ratio is altered in favor of the emotional life in family drawings. The figures will tend to show some degree of regression when compared to the previously drawn single person. Like grown-ups, children perform more "sensibly" when the emotions are in check.

11

CONCEPT AND OBJECT RELATIONS

The breakdown of behavior into its component parts facilitates description and investigation. The child, however, functions as a unit from the very beginning of life. All functions are interrelated and interdependent. In normal individuals sensation, motion, perception, cognition, and emotion are all functions of an integrated whole. Among the various facets of the personality, the relationship between intelligence and affectivity is basic. It grows during the early months and becomes the foundation from which the personality derives stability and health.

Though each recognized affectivity and intelligence as inseparable aspects of the whole, S. Freud did not concern himself with cognitive development, and Piaget was concerned with epistemology without looking at affectivity. Granted that a relationship exists between these two crucial aspects of the personality, just how are they related? How do they correspond in time and sequence? These questions have resulted in theoretical formulations and, more recently, in experimental investigation. Of special interest is the study conducted by Gouin Décarie (1965) on 90 subjects between the ages of three and 20 months. The investigation focused on the object as conceived by Piaget and on object relations as viewed by Freudian ego psychologists, and, more precisely, on the relationship between the cognitive and libidinal object. Conducted within an experimental setting, the study tends to support her working hypothesis of a close link between the two, despite the differences that prevail in the definition of object by the Piagetian and Freudian theorists.

The "object" according to Piaget

Fundamental to the integration of cognition and affectivity is the development of the object concept. First, it is necessary to define what is meant by object concept. According to Piaget, one may speak of "object" when something in the external world can not only be seen, heard, and touched but when it exists even when not present in the perceptual field. Until this concept is achieved, the universe of the child is radically different from that of the adult. The notion of permanency is apparent when the child searches actively for a vanished object.

Piaget identifies five steps in the development of the object concept. These stages cover the period from birth to 18-20 months, the approximate age when most children will have achieved the concept of permanence. Recognition precedes by many months the concept of permanence. The infant recognizes the mother's face at four months but "loses" her when she leaves his perceptual field, that is, when he can no longer see, or hear, or touch her. This fact is often clearly manifested by the crying that ensues when mother leaves the perceptual field—a crying that immediately subsides when she makes her presence known visually or acoustically. Piaget interprets this behavior as indicating "affective permanence" and distinguishes it from "objective permanence" which he regards as the true concept of permanence of objects. As the infant approaches the ninth month, the beginnings of search for the vanished object may be seen in his attempt to remove an obstacle to the desired object.

The "object" in the context of Freudian psychoanalysis

All that is the *not I* constitutes the world of objects. In the context of object relations, the object is essentially the infant's first love object, the nurturing adult. Just as in Piaget's theory of the development of object concept, psychoanalysis identifies steps or sequences in the development of object relations as subject and object interact. In the beginning, the infant is said to have no awareness of the outside. During the course of the first year, the infant gradually becomes aware of the existence of external objects, notably the mother. As the infant's ego emerges, it slowly assumes the functions hitherto performed by the mothering figure. By the time the child is 18 months of age, he is quite aware of the distinction between *self* and *non-self* as cathexis is transferred from self to object. The affective tie to the mother is preceded by pleasure derived from the creature comforts (food, cuddling), which only after the sixth month begin to be associated with the "giver" in whose perceptual context the good things are consistently received.

My own observations suggest that the infant "objectifies" body parts, including his own, before he becomes aware that they are but parts of the self or of another whole. I have observed repeatedly that infants under nine months of age will not turn to look for the person standing behind when they see the person's hand. The hand is an object from the external world but it does not appear as indicating the presence of a person who is not in the perceptual field.

Object constancy

There is general agreement that prolonged institutionalization of infants and young children (of anyone, for that matter) adversely affects their personality. In the case of the very young, the effects tend to abide.

Two hypotheses are stressed for the explanation of the deleterious effects: one relates it primarily, if not exclusively, to insufficient sensory and/or perceptual stimulation; the other to absence of maternal care. Alpert and Di Leo have offered a third hypothesis: that object constancy, with appropriate stimulation as an integral part of it, is the crucial need of infancy (first two years of life) for normal development.

By object constancy is meant that the same person ministers to the child's needs for most of the day and most every day, thus establishing a reciprocal, interacting system between the child and the caretaking adult. This does not exclude the sharing of some lesser part of the nurturing role by other persons as frequently occurs in average home care, particularly in extended families.

It is assumed that object constancy is not just a quantitative term, but implies also a higher degree of warmth in the mothering figure, as a by-product of the favorable adult-child ratio (except for unmaternal women, a variable present in homes as well as in institutions). Alpert and Di Leo hypothecated that full social development, especially speech and communication and social adaptation, is strongly susceptible precisely to the constancy of the relationship with a mothering person and that, if this is so, it would point the way to safeguarding an appreciable percentage of our resources at the time of their highest potential. "I have found that the capacity for object relations is the ego function which, together with the self-image, suffers most damage when maternal deprivation has been experienced in the first years of childhood" (Alpert, 1965).

Alpert has shown that pathological fixations associated with maternal deficiency can be alleviated in large measure through restitution by symbolic object constancy in prelatency children. On the basis of these findings, she hypothecated that the application of object constancy at younger age levels would safeguard the child's development, and would serve as a prophylactic agent for institutionalized infants. In his long experience with these infants, Di Leo had shared with Alpert his observation that head banging and rocking had all but disappeared with reduction in the nurse-baby ratio and greater interaction between the infants and greater consistency in type of care and stimulation. The infants became more responsive to the human object and less involved in self-stimulation when fewer nurses gave care.

A research project devised to provide a greater measure of object constancy within institutions was to be conducted jointly by Alpert and Di Leo. Unfortunately, the project ran into administrative difficulties that could not be resolved at the time. However, long clinical experience has shown this author that maturational lags and deviations resulting from maternal deprivation were often favorably modified after placement in families and that the effects of deprivation were directly related to the duration of deprivation. Even without systematic investigation of the question, most would probably agree that object constancy during infancy would tend to increase the child's ability to respond to the human object.

Reversibility of pathological fixations

Undeterred by pessimistic pronouncements, the late Augusta Alpert, after carefully studying the problems, evolved a therapeutic procedure aimed at localizing the point of traumatic fixation. This entailed an "unwinding of the developmental reel" with further regression until the early distortions and etiological elements were exposed. The teacher in an exclusive relationship with the child offers gratification and satisfaction of the early unmet needs and gradually leads the child beyond that primitive level to growth in object relations beyond need satisfaction. In three cases published, Alpert (1959) succeeded in reversing the pathological effects so that the children began to enjoy their childhood for the first time. All these children had shown severe disturbances in object relations, especially with adults. Behavior ranged from hostile rejection to autistic withdrawal. They were erroneously considered to be schizophrenic children but with a difference. Although they were not institution children, all had suffered early maternal deprivation. These were all severely traumatized children presenting serious disorders of personality. And yet, it was possible to bring about a significant improvement in ego structure.

My experience over long years supports the serious hazards of prolonged institutionalization, but I do not share the pessimism expressed by many and the hopelessness that it engenders. Infants vary even in their capacity to sustain deprivation and in their ability to rebound even after prolonged deprivation. Constitutional factors probably account for the variation in stress resistance and resilience. The fact is that the differences do exist. And to demonstrate it are the many teenage boys and girls and the many adults who, despite prolonged institutionalization, were able to emerge and enter the cultural mainstream as functioning, contributing members of their community.

PART TWO

The World as Seen Through the Eyes of Children

12

WE SPEAK TO CHILDREN

We speak to children. But how much and what do they understand of what we are saying?

During the first months of life, we speak to them through the sense of touch. They, in turn, understand nothing but feel and sense a good deal. They sense our moods and attitudes, whether we love them or tolerate them. In this empathetic exchange lies the groundwork for a pleasurable or disturbing relationship. Throughout the years, I have seen how babies cared for by distraught teenage mothers would react with gastrointestinal disorders that had no basis in organic dysfunction, that yielded to no change in formula or medication, but that ceased promptly when care was turned over to a nurse who had no emotional involvement in the unpleasant social situation of which the baby was the concrete symbol.

Before they understand our adult words, children can comprehend the deeper structures of our speech from the tone, facial expression, and gestures that are often more telling than the spoken word. Indeed, they have an uncanny ability to detect the hidden meaning behind the adult's verbal camouflage.

In the development of language, comprehension of speech precedes its expressive use. Just how the child acquires word meanings continues to be a fascinating area of investigation. The evidence points to two principal ways by which children learn to decode adult verbal symbols: at first, directly, by association of the word they hear with an object or person in their perceptual field; later, indirectly, from the context in which the new word is heard. In the earlier way, the adult says the word, while the child sees or touches the object. In the indirect way, the meaning is detected from the verbal context in which the new word is embedded. This is a later stage, since it implies comprehension of the matrix. In this case, the child infers the meaning from contextual clues.

Werner and Kaplan (1950) devised a Word Context Test aimed at determining the child's ability to acquire meaning from context. The test uses artificial words such as "hudray, contavish, prignatus" inserted into sentences. The meaning of the strange word can be acquired from the context.

Knowing how children learn meanings of words is of great value not only to the speech therapist but to all parents. Much over-talking can be avoided when parents realize the child's normal developmental limitations of comprehension. It has also been noted that comprehension in young children is more dependent upon affective tone and context than on the actual speech patterns used by the adult.

In progressing from words to sentences, ability to decode is influenced by psychological and linguistic features that bear upon the syntactic and semantic aspects of sentences.

Early verbal exchange between mother and child

Brown and Bellugi (1964) investigated the development of English syntax in children between 18 and 36 months of age. Among the findings of this classic longitudinal study is the frequent occurrence of imitation of the mother's speech with reduction by the child, and imitation of the child's speech with expansion by the mother. A few examples:

Direct imitation: *Mother:* "Daddy's car"
Child: "Daddy car"

Imitation with reduction: *Mother:* "The doggie is hungry."
Child: "Doggie hungry"

Imitation with expansion: *Child:* "Doggie there"
Mother: "The doggie is there."

In a recent study of verbal interaction in two- and three-year-olds and their mothers, Reichle, Longhurst, and Stepanich (1976) reported that reduction to telegraphic speech was prominent in two-year-olds and that three-year-olds were less dependent on imitation and more inclined to initiate interaction by asking questions. Mothers of the older children used longer, more complex sentences that added additional information to the child's utterance.

Child: "Doggie there"
Mother: "The doggie has a black nose and long ears."

There are innumerable amusing anecdotes of how children interpret and render what they are taught: ". . . and lead us not into Penn Station, . . ." may or may not be what the child actually said in reciting the Lord's Prayer, but I can vividly recall the kindergartner giving the Pledge of Allegiance to "one nation invisible . . .". One wonders what goes through the young mind that is confronted with terms intended to express abstract ideas far beyond its understanding (see Figure 12).

A recent study by Nelson indicated that children between the ages of 5½ and 9½ were better able to comprehend spoken language when speaking rate was reduced and sentences were less complex. Comprehension, as expected, improved with age. All this is but another confirmation of what has been known intuitively.

In communicating with children one should be aware of their limitations. Specifically, one should be aware of their vague concepts of time, space, and number, concepts that are beyond the cognition of most two-year-olds. At that age, children live in the here and now. When we tell the naughty child "wait till your father comes home," we must admit that when that event does occur, the connection between the misdeed and the promised punishment will have been completely lost. At two, time is *now;* "later" is, at best, the immediate future. "Wait" can last but a few minutes. The difference between morning and afternoon will remain vague until the end of the preschool years.

The child of two lives in a limited radius with *self* at the center and will continue to radiate out from self throughout the preschool years. Directions will be understood and complied with only when they are expressed in concrete terms: "put the ball on the *chair*," or "on the *table*," or "give it to *me*" will be complied with because of the concrete word, the noun. But the direction "put the ball *under*" or "*in front of* the chair" will not be understood because the key word is a preposition that expresses a concept of space that is beyond the child's understanding at the two-year level of maturity. Too often, failure to comprehend is misinterpreted as stubbornness or willful disobedience.

The years two, three, and four are critical years in more ways than one. They are critical because of the abiding shape that is being assumed by the personality; critical because behavior that was tolerated when the child was a nonverbal infant is now becoming an expression of individuality in both word and action. Parent and child are often of two minds. Parents bur-

FIGURE 12

Carolyn B., an intelligent child of six, attended a Good Friday Worship Service and was so impressed by the account of the death of Jesus that she drew the scene.

It is a highly original rendition of Jesus on the Cross and it is certainly at variance with the image that the Minister had tried to convey.

This is but another example of a child's own way of interpreting the language of adults. The word "on" has been pictured literally and correctly though not as intended by the speaker.

We are often not very successful in getting our message across to children—at least not until they are seven or eight.

A long, involved story about unfamiliar events is likely to confuse, where a picture would be far more effective in creating a clear mental image.

(The drawing is reproduced by permission of the Rev. Ian D. G. Brown of Rosanna, Victoria, Australia.)

FIGURE 12

dened by affliction and stress may not appreciate the child's expressions of freedom. The inability to make the "proper" decision between alternatives, the frequent use of the word *"no,"* and the resistance to forced feeding and to habit-training are not understood by the parent as signs of healthy emotional phases. It is during these years that parental anger is vented upon the child in physical abuse or in subtle, but equally disastrous, psychological rejection.

Arts in early development

The arts can play a most effective role in contributing to the intellectual, emotional, and aesthetic life of children. Music, pantomime, and the visual arts can supplement and, on occasion, surpass the spoken word as media of communication. The visual arts in particular are valuable because of their unique attribute of presenting their content at once. In verbal communication, content must be stretched out over a period of time. The same is true of the other art forms: music, dance, and drama. In painting, composition, color, and relationships are simultaneously presented to the viewer. A verbal or written description, requiring numerous sentences and paragraphs, might not achieve the same effect.

Comprehension in the stage of concrete operations

The profound shift in cognitive functioning that occurs at about seven or eight years is manifest also in the comprehension and use of language. Heretofore, during the preoperational period, problems were solved motorically, by trial and error, thinking was dominated by perception, things were taken at face value, and, accordingly, language was expressive of the here and now. Now, with the advent of concrete operations, logic is less dependent upon the presently available information, so that concepts of conservation can be acquired despite irrelevant changes in shape, weight, and size. Language during this period will express the concrete character of the child's logic. The comprehension and proper use of abstract terms must await the next level of cognitive functioning, that of formal operations. Many children with learning disabilities continue to think and consequently express themselves in concrete terms well beyond third grade.

Myklebust (1954), in relating language to experience, has identified the following sequence: sensation, perception, symbolization, and, finally, conceptualization. This sequence corresponds essentially to Piaget's stages. In the development of speech, a bicycle will be defined at first as something with two wheels, then as something you ride, and eventually as a vehicle. An apple is seen as something round, something red, something you eat, and, only later, as a fruit.

In drawing, transparencies disappear as the child draws his internalized images. In drawing a man in a boat, the child after age seven or eight will no longer show parts of the body through the hull. He will probably laugh when shown his earlier drawings and may even deny that he could do such a silly thing.

Informing the adopted child

There is general agreement that an adopted child must be made aware of the fact that he is adopted. I have known a few parents who have withheld the information from the child. They have lived in dread of the inevitable moment of truth. Their anxiety is surpassed only by the shock sustained by the adoptee who has been living in ignorant bliss regarding his status and belatedly discovers that those are not natural parents.

Some overly zealous adopting parents have started using the word "adoption" to the baby with the intent of accustoming the infant to its sound. But it is not really until three or four that the child can acquire some familiarity with the term. During the preschool years, the situation becomes entangled with the basic facts of reproduction. "Where do babies come from?" or, more pointedly, "Where did *I* come from?"

In my experience it is usually at about seven or eight that the child becomes aware of the two mothers. As comprehension grows, the child may want to know more. Some loving adopting parents, intending to stress the fact that, though not naturally theirs, the child is appreciated, wanted, and dearly loved, have told a story of how they, being childless, went to a place where there were hundreds of babies in need of a family, and that on seeing their child, they immediately recognized the one that they wanted above all others. One child asked about the natural mother and was told that she loved him exceedingly but could not care for him herself and so, reluctantly, entrusted him to the care of those who would love him and prepare for his future. The child listened silently. At the end his only comment was "Do you mean somebody had me and just gave me away?"

The adopting parents are well advised to respond to the growing child's need to know by offering some facts about the natural mother or parents, if they know. It is helpful to tell the child of her appearance, occupation, and talents so as not to leave all to the child's fantasy. It is generally the absent biological mother that most evokes confusion and the need to know. The natural father is more likely to be ignored as "a man of no importance."

Informing the child in foster care

The difficulty of offering an acceptable explanation to the child in foster care is compounded when the child is in temporary care. As this situation is prolonged, and the child matures, an account will have to be given of the unfortunate circumstances that led to placement in a foster home. The temporary nature of the placement tends to tear away at any substantial sense of security and self-esteem. How can one explain the situation to those children who have been transferred from home to home? Eventually the child will ask why his surname and that of the foster family are different (a fact that does not escape the attention of his peers). The child must be told the truth. Gradually, he will put the pieces together. Criticism of the natural parents must be avoided, whatever their shortcomings. Many children have grown out of their foster home into the community, and have maintained an affectionate relationship with the foster family.

In any case, what really matters is the atmosphere that prevails in the home that is providing care. When children are young, meanings are comprehended before words. It is only later that words can shape meanings. Communicating the bitter truth to socially displaced children requires tact, understanding, and affectionate regard. The truth must be told kindly so that it may hurt less.

In institutionalized children, relationships tend to be superficial. Questions may never be asked. The whole matter of why and where to is likely to be an ignored reality. Except in unusual cases requiring residential care, life in a congregate shelter is poor preparation for the world without.

Regardless of how understandably and compassionately the knowledge of their condition has been imparted to adopted, foster or institutionalized children, one should be prepared for identity problems far above and beyond those generally encountered in children reared by their own natural parents. The lack of roots into the past poses a serious threat to the youth's emotional stability and self-image. The ambiguity that surrounds origins is particularly disturbing at adolescence when the need becomes intense to know "Who am I? Where do I belong?" The favorable resolution of this critical stage depends upon what has happened during the earlier years in structuring the personality.

While it is generally true that the welfare of children is in the following descending order of environmental influences: own parents—adoptive parents—foster parents—institution, this is by no means a valid rule of thumb applicable to all. Nor is a "good" surrogate parent necessarily better for the child than his own "bad" parent. More than once, I have seen a child, who had been separated from an abusing parent, literally jump into her arms and hug and kiss her avidly when she came to visit. After all, that is the child's mother, the only one he has. It takes a great deal to alter an image, even though it be more a fiction than any semblance of reality. The child in placement must not hear any criticism of his parents. He needs to know that they love him and that his foster parents respect them. Eventually, their concern and their real feelings will become manifest, as parental visits become less frequent and end altogether, as is commonly the case.

13

CHILDREN SPEAK TO US

In conformity with lawful growth, language proceeds from the general to the particular. During the period from 12 to 18 months, the child acquires a vocabulary of about a dozen single words. These words are really word-sentences (McCarthy, 1954), having many meanings that can be divined from the context and inflection. "Ball" may be said to mean "give me the ball," "where is the ball?" "take the ball," etc. In the same way, "man" or "dog" may be applied indiscriminately. As an example, one day in the subway, a child sitting on his mother's lap pointed to a man sitting across and called "daddy" to the amusement of the passengers and some embarrassment to the mother.

Family members, and especially older siblings, may be so adept at interpreting the infant's wants and needs that they may actually block the development of speech. There are instances in which overprotective mind-reading mothers decrease the child's incentive to speak for himself. Similarly, delayed speech has been noted in twins who develop their own jargon, with which they effectively communicate with each other.

In the normal course of language development, words are gradually applied less widely; "bow-wow" becomes restricted to dog and not, as previously, to any quadruped. Names are attached to specific individuals. Words will be associated with concepts. But even as the child grows older, words and sentences may not communicate concepts that in themselves are ill-defined. The whole process of education has been defined as a process of clarification of concept—and this is a lifelong process. The adult is well advised to keep this in mind especially when young children are speaking.

Before age six or seven, speech is but another manifestation of the egocentricity that dominates all aspects of behavior. Words are repeated for their own sake, often in an echolalic way, just for the joy of producing and hearing them. They are used as commands or expressions of desires but not really to communicate thought. The child may talk in the presence of another child but not to tell him anything. It is as though he were talking to himself, a phenomenon that is of common occurrence in many adults. The young child talks without taking into account the point of view of the other.

It is not until the child emerges from the stage of egocentricity that language takes on a socialized function in which thoughts are exchanged.

The function of language is not merely to communicate thought. It is often used to obscure thought or to prevent it from being communicated. Children may resort to lying as a defense. But, on the other hand, what sounds like lying may be simply an attempt to give expression with limited verbal means to a view that is necessarily different from the adult's.

Much parental mismanagement results from failure to realize that the child's language does not mean to him what it means to us—and, I might add, that what we say will not be understood as intended, certainly not during the preschool years.

It is well to bear these considerations in mind before taking what young children say at face value. The child's actions tell more clearly than his words what he thinks and feels. The inner voices of children are better seen than heard.

The "no" is not always a "no"

One of the most trying periods for both parent and child is the phase of resistance or negativism that occurs in two- and three-year-olds. To a greater or lesser degree it is experienced by all healthy children in their progress toward emotional maturity. Resistance is already seen in the neonate who struggles against restraint. But only after six months is the resistance directed against another person, for it is only now that a beginning awareness of a non-self is entering the infant's consciousness. With the achievement of a concept of object relations during the second year, aided and abetted by the freedom to move about and the acquisition of expressive language, assertiveness can become active opposition. Studies have shown that during this period of so-called negativism, the word *"no"* is spoken more than three times as often as "yes." This *"no"* to almost every parental demand is irritating to many parents who do not understand its many meanings. I submit that when a child stands squarely on his feet, looks the parent in the eye and says *"no,"* the situation calls for rejoicing. Its real meaning is that the child is asserting an individuality that is a most desirable asset of the personality. Does the parent want a person or a compliant dummy? This is not advocating anarchy. Of çourse, limits should be drawn to unbridled self-expression. But within a framework limited to what is dangerous or really disruptive, the child should be allowed considerable freedom of verbal and motor expression.

This opens up the whole fascinating field of communication. Do even we adults really understand what we are saying to each other? Rilke tells us that infinite distances exist even between the closest human beings. Does not each of us interpret what we see and hear within the context of our past, present, and our vision of the future? How then can we assume that our message is getting across to the child in its unaltered, pristine content?

To the child, the word *"no"* that he uses so frequently must have a variety of meanings, many of them unassociated with defiance. It may very well be (and I know it to be so in many instances) that the child's *"no"* is but an imitation or identification with the parent whose notion of child training consists in an unending series of *"don'ts."* The negativism which is a healthy phase in the organization of personality may become entrenched as a permanent trait through parental misunderstanding and a resolve to break it, thinking that, "If he defies me at three, what will he do at 16?"

Limited in vocabulary, the child's *"no"* may be his way of saying "don't rush me; wait," just as he may say "I don't" when he cares very much indeed and is simply trying to save face. Every loving parent can tell an amusing tale of her child's misinterpretation of what she thought she had explained so clearly. Attempts to impart sex instruction to young children are replete with misinterpretations, particularly when metaphors are used instead of simple, direct language.

When the child is faced with alternatives, choice is difficult and it may not be the one desired by the parent. In training, greater emphasis should be placed on rewarding and less on punishment—more "do's" and very few if any "don'ts."

If the adult would take a moment to do a little role-playing, to adopt the viewpoint of the child, it would become quite evident how disagreeable it must be to be washed, combed, and encased in "proper" clothing when everything inside is clamoring for action and nakedness. Cultural restraints have little attraction. The *"no"* is a yearning for a freer state and not a lust for power.

Negative emotions tend to distort thinking. Instructions given in a simple, specific form and in a pleasant tone are better understood than general, verbose directions imparted in a tone of reprimand.

Piaget has directed considerable attention to the questions asked by young children, believing them to be expressions of the child's level of thought. He distinguishes three broad types and relates them to stages in cognitive development. The first two types, *questions of causal explanation* (about physical phenomena, objects, machines), and *questions of motivation* (about the activities of human beings), are asked with increasing frequency between three and seven years. *Questions of logical justification* (rules of language, spelling, social conventions, mathematical concepts) are very rare before the age of seven or eight. Before that stage, the child is not interested in logical justification; he asserts without proving. Questions like "why is 4.5 half of 9?" are indicative ot logical reasoning and do not come to mind before the stage of concrete operations. It is within this conceptual framework that I have made the statement that it is futile to engage in logical reasoning (as we adults understand it) with children before they are about seven or eight years of age.

Inner voices

In her recent book, Despert vividly points out the discrepancy between the inner and outer voices of children. It is unlikely that the child's speech will accurately express the thoughts intended. ". . . the inner voices hardly need words, . . ." (Despert, 1975).

"Drawings are less susceptible than speech to the influence of defenses. More than words can tell, they are valuable aids to understanding the child and his problems" (Di Leo, 1970). In my books on children's drawings I have advised against asking specific questions about the drawing. Ask questions and one gets answers. By asking "what is it?" and similar questions, we are influencing ". . . a premature connection between two areas of development that are at different levels of maturity. The three-year-old is at the very threshold of graphic representation while already well advanced in language development" (Di Leo, 1970).

I am well aware that psychologists attach considerable value to information derived from interview and discussion. I recognize the value of verbal exchange with the child. What I am saying is simply that the questions should be of a general nature, for example: "Tell me something about your drawing." I should also like to make it clear that in advising "the less said, the better," I have in mind those who are not professionals in the fields of child development. Yet, even a highly skilled interviewer may agree with Piaget that in questioning a child it is hard not to talk too much, to avoid suggesting the response.

Children may speak to us more clearly and openly through their drawings than they are willing or able to do verbally. There is something very personal about one's drawing, especially if the subject is the human figure, alone or as part of a family group.

Certain overall characteristics of children's drawings tend to correlate with personality traits. The secure child usually draws freely, utilizing the available space, with good firm pressure and continuity of stroke. In contrast, the insecure child's drawing will be small, restricted to a small area of the available space, and the lines will be lightly drawn, often broken or wavering.

But apart from these general features, the attention of observers has been focused on specific items because they are often omitted, exaggerated, or unusual. Reference is made to the feelings of inadequacy or of not belonging in the child who excludes himself from his drawing of the family. Timidity is suggested when the child draws a figure with absent or rudimentary arms and hands. Tiny unstable feet are interpreted as expressions of insecurity. Grotesque, disjointed figures are a frequent feature in drawings by children with serious emotional disorders. Excessive shading is seen as an indicator of anxiety.

So far, one is still within the area of wide agreement as regards interpretation. But the drawings may be telling us more. The interpretation now becomes increasingly subjective, more open to differences of opinion. Opinion is not knowledge. Yet, even so, the drawings remain, with the Rorschach, the most widely used among the projective techniques. Many, but by no means all, the indicators described by Machover (1949) have withstood the test of statistical analysis. She has defined the following items as sexual symbols: the hair, hat, shoe, pipe, cigarette, gun. Other features that refer to personality structure, besides those already mentioned, are aggressive or depressed stance of the figure, rigidity, compulsive symmetry, incompletion, and repeated erasures.

In drawings by children old enough to portray members of the family each doing something (Burns and Kaufman, 1970), the child often reveals the nature of a problem that is rooted in the complex transactions within the family group. The recurrence of certain items to which the authors attach symbolic significance is regarded as suggestive of well-defined syndromes. Among these items are lamps, vacuum cleaners, stoves, ironing boards, and lawn mowers.

As children grow older, they are increasingly influenced by the culture, a fact that is reflected in their drawings. Now, more than ever before, one must avoid jumping to conclusions from insufficient evidence. The drawings are only a part of the diagnostic process. They are a valuable, and, at times, an indispensable aid to a diagnosis that must rest on comprehensive investigation.

Because of the subjective element in interpreting drawings, their value as a projective technique is bound to encounter skepticism from those who demand scientific verification. Undoubtedly, the validity of interpretation is directly related to the skill and experience of the clinician. We are not dealing with an automatic testing device. We do not discard the stethoscope because there are varying degrees of skill in interpreting the information it conveys.

Less controversial is the use of drawings as indicators of intelligence. The work of Goodenough (1926) and Harris (1963) provides a firm experimental and statistical base for their validity.

Drawings are of considerable clinical value as indicators of neurological dysfunction or organicity. Since the original observations by Schilder (1950) and Bender (1940), others, including the present writer, have confirmed the disparity between concept of body image and intellectual capacity in children who present clinically with signs of neurological deficit. The concept of body image in these children is significantly below intellectual capacity as determined from standardized psychological tests such as the Stanford-Binet.

FIGURE 13

Valentine to mother by six-year-old boy.

FIGURE 14

Three wishes by Donna, age 7½.
Girls are generally more articulate than boys and tend to express themselves verbally and in writing as well as in their drawings.

By their drawings, children can reveal their aspirations, preferences, and attitudes. Dennis (1966) goes even further and states that they reflect "not only the values of children but also the values of their societies."

The two drawings **(Figures 15 and 16)** that follow, one by a girl of eight, the other by a boy of twelve, communicate the social roles admired and desired. Communication is more direct, immediate, and total than with the spoken word. The boy did not offer a verbal comment on his football hero. The girl added, "That's what I want to be when I grow up." She explained that the *H* on the building stood for *hospital*.

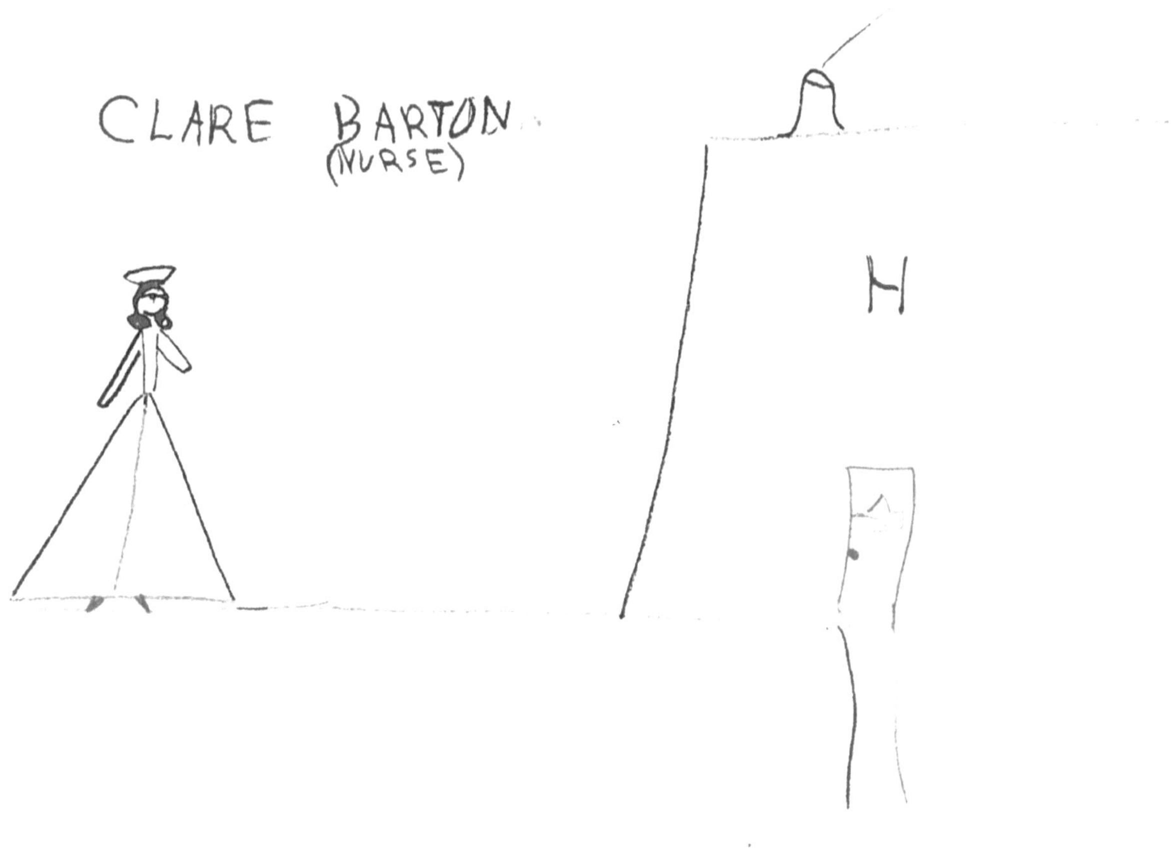

FIGURE 15

FIGURE 16

At age 7 this bright girl tells that she will dance on her toes when she is 10 (**Figure 17**).

She is quite clear as to what she wants to do. And so, a year and a half later, she specifies that she wishes to be a ballerina (**Figure 18**). The figure has acquired grace and beauty.

FIGURE 17

"When I am ten years old."

FIGURE 18

FIGURE 19

Having finished her drawing of a Princess, this eight-year-old added, "That's what I would like to be." Symbolic wish fulfillment?

FIGURE 20

Spontaneous drawing by girl of eleven years. She is in a residential center for school-age children. She has drawn a house. There are no windows. There are no persons in the drawing. Does she want a home?

I have seen many drawings by children in need of a home. Many of them have spontaneously drawn houses.

FIGURE 21

Spontaneous drawing by a girl of 7½ years. Average intelligence. She is in a foster home. Children wanting a permanent home often draw houses. The foster family is considering adopting the child. Her comment about the drawing: "It's raining, but the sun is going to clear." There are darkened sun and raindrops, but flowers are an optimistic note.

FIGURE 22

This drawing expresses good adjustment of adopted child. Drawing by an adopted boy of nine years. This is a pleasant scene in which all members, including himself, are present. The house is emphasized, drawn first. The smoke issuing from the chimney indicates warmth. The sun is shining on the happy occasion. "All had a party and the guests went home. We all went out to say good-bye to them."

FIGURE 23

Spontaneous drawing by a girl of ten years.

Rejected by her natural mother, this child was cared for in a residential nursery. Between age three and seven she had been in three foster homes. In each placement, she had exhibited disruptive, aggressive behavior directed mainly against the foster mother, to a degree that resulted in the families' refusal to continue care. In the last of her three placements she had begun to make a fair adjustment when she was returned to the agency because the family had decided to move to a distant location and was not disposed to take her along. The child, now seven, was deeply hurt, interpreting the event as another instance of rejection. Anger and hostility became more intense. Psychiatric evaluation ascribed her behavior to deep-seated "anger towards own mother, which she takes out on any mother surrogate."

In studying her drawing the following items draw attention: 1) there are no persons; 2) the sky is darkened and there are clouds; 3) part of the sun is shining; 4) there are large flowers; 5) a small house is off to one side, partly out of the scene; 6) a tree dominates the scene. It is on the right. The crown is small and closed. The tree has no roots. The trunk is cut off at the bottom. There is a scar above the mid-level.

Viewing the scene as a projection of the child's personality, one may interpret the items as meaningful expressions of feelings and attitudes.

The absence of persons occurs frequently in drawings by socially-displaced children. "It is so unusual for young children to omit persons from their drawings as to justify consideration of probable difficulty in interpersonal relationships" (Di Leo, 1973). Clouds and darkened sky: "These ominous signs have been seen in drawings by unhappy children." (ibid).

Sun shining, though only a part, as well as the presence of large flowers would indicate hope in an otherwise dismal situation. The small house, partly out of the picture, suggests abiding interest in a home though it may be fading.

The symbolism of the tree has been the subject of much theorizing and speculation. The tree in this drawing has no roots, the trunk is definitely cut off at its base. These features may symbolize the child's lack of a family. The scar suggests a deep hurt. The location of the scar may indicate the time when the trauma occurred. According to Buck (1948), the height of the tree represents the subject's age. In this particular drawing, the location of the scar above the mid-level would place the traumatic event at about age six. Placement of the tree far over to the right has been interpreted as an expression of rejection of maternal influence. The small, closed crown is indicative of restricted social life and aspirations.

This is by no means the only way in which the perceptual material of the drawing may be interpreted; nor is that all that can be said about it. The reader may reject it as far-fetched or may regard it as superficial or overly restrained.

FIGURE 23

FIGURE 24

Drawing of her family by an adopted girl age 12½ years. She has omitted herself from the family group. This is not unusual in adopted children. The search for an identity may be critical and frustrating during the adolescent years. She has been in the home since early infancy.

This carefully made drawing reflects a meticulous, tidy, exact, perfectionist. She is in 7th grade. In her verbal comment she states that she has many friends.

The figures in the drawing are static. All hands are concealed, a feature that has been interpreted as indicating guilt. I suggest that it may perhaps be a device used by a perfectionistic child to bypass a task at which she may not succeed. It is difficult to draw hands properly.

FIGURE 25

Drawn by a 10½ year-old boy.
He has placed "Pop" and himself on pedestals.

Emotionally traumatic effects of separation from the mother are clearly evident after the age of six months. A sense of loss may be manifested by striking changes in behavior, such as are seen in children who have been removed from their parents or abandoned by them and admitted to residential nurseries. There is no uniform pattern. I have seen depression, hostility, indiscriminate clinging, regression, and auto-erotic activity to the exclusion of any involvement with the new environment. Notably hazardous, and yet to a certain extent preventable, is the trauma resulting from hospitalization. A preschooler left in a hospital cannot accept or comprehend that what is done is for his own good. Potential trauma can be prevented by permitting the parent to remain in hospital with the child in a rooming-in arrangement. There is consensus that such facilities are needed but very few hospitals do more than give lip-service to this crucial problem. There is good evidence that the traumatic effects of hospitalization, interpreted by the child as rejection or abandonment, can have long-term sequelae.

Figure 26, drawn by a boy of six, clearly expresses his feelings towards mother. In this verbal comments, he tells the reasons for his hospitalization as he interprets them. No amount of "reasoning" will alter the fact that he was brought there and left there. Again, it is not what we adults do or say that really matters, but how what we do or say is interpreted by the child. Feelings of rejection or abandonment cut deeply. Children in hospitals should be encouraged to give expression to their feelings, and drawing is a most valuable medium for the release of pent-up, destructive feelings.

Impressed by the large number of adolescents in guidance clinics who had a history of hospitalization during their preschool years, Douglas (1975) undertook a study to determine whether the two events were related. This careful study of hundreds of adolescents "provides strong and unexpected evidence that one admission to hospital of more than a week's duration or repeated admissions before the age of five years (in particular between six months and four years) are associated with an increased risk of behavior disturbance and poor reading in adolescence." Those most vulnerable were those most dependent on mother and those under stress (sibling rivalry, insecurity, mother's entry to work coinciding with hospitalization). The recommendation is that children be admitted with their mothers, if possible.

FIGURE 26

Drawing and commentary by a hospitalized boy, age six (reproduced by courtesy of Mr. David Fassler).
"This is a picture of my mother when she was a monster."
Doctor: "When was she a monster?"
"When she wanted to chase me out of the house."
Doctor: "Why did she want you out of the house?"
"She doesn't like me. She wants me to stay in the hospital."
Doctor: "Why do you think she wants you to stay in the hospital?"
"She only wants one son.'
Doctor: "I think she really loves you."
"No! She told me she only wants one son."

The Australian Association for the Welfare of Children in Hospital has recommended that no child shall be kept in hospital any longer than is absolutely necessary; that parental access to children should not be limited; that facilities for rooming-in should be provided; and that all staff be trained in the psychological needs of children. These recommendations have the support of the government (*The Lancet,* 1975).

Image of the father

Though in different ways, the father is a determining influence in the emotional life of both girls and boys. His influence becomes increasingly manifest after the age of two. During the preschool years, the boy's attachment to his father and admiration for his superior powers alternate with anxiety arising from rivalry for possession of the mother. In girls, love and admiration for the father generate a desire to supplant the mother as the object of his affection.

Absence of the father from the family constellation, where there is no adequate substitute, deprives the child of an important influence in the formation of character and personality. Paternal influence is directly related to quality of the relationship and not to the actual time the father is present. The child's vivid fantasy fills the time gap. If there is a known father, the fantasy stems from a reality; where there is no flesh-and-blood father, the child will tend to invent one.

Those of us who work among children without families are struck by the intensity with which fatherless children try to attach themselves to a benevolent adult male. In institutions, the personnel is female to an excessively preponderant, albeit unavoidable, degree. When an adult male appears, the children will suspend their activities and stare at the visitor. As all eyes are turned in his direction, the more venturesome will approach, touch, even clutch the man's arm and possessively declare "he's mine."

My long experience with these children has confirmed the sensitive and perceptive observations of Anna Freud and Dorothy Burlingham on young children separated from their families during the barbarism of the Second World War. Particularly touching are the children's refusal to accept the fact of the father's death, their insistence that he will return because he is big

FIGURE 27

Drawing of his family by a 12½ year-old child. He is doing well at school and is entering 8th grade.

The following is his description of the scene: "This is my family going on our summer vacation—we are each carrying our own suitcases filled with our clothes—on our little trip we will cook out—my whole family is excited about our trip, especially Mom and Dad."

(There is no father in the home. The father died almost ten years ago. Father has no mouth suggesting silence.)

and strong, the claim of having seen him walking on the street, the intensity with which fantasy pervades reality and causes one to ask the perennial question, "What is reality?"

In the case of the absent father, or the one who visits sporadically, one is impressed by the aforementioned striking disproportion between the importance of the father in the child's mind and the limited, meagre time spent with him. Often, in my experience, where custody has been given to the mother, the boy will blame her for the separation, resulting in bitterness directed at her, coupled with lack of motivation and failure at school despite even superior intellectual capacity, and general free-floating hostility.

It is my belief that the father's role should not remain vacant.

FIGURE 28

Drawn by boy of seven. The parents separated just prior to his birth. Father visits regularly. The boy blames his mother. He attends first grade. Presenting problem: hostility towards girls, hits them. Mothers of the girls have complained to school authorities.

FIGURE 28

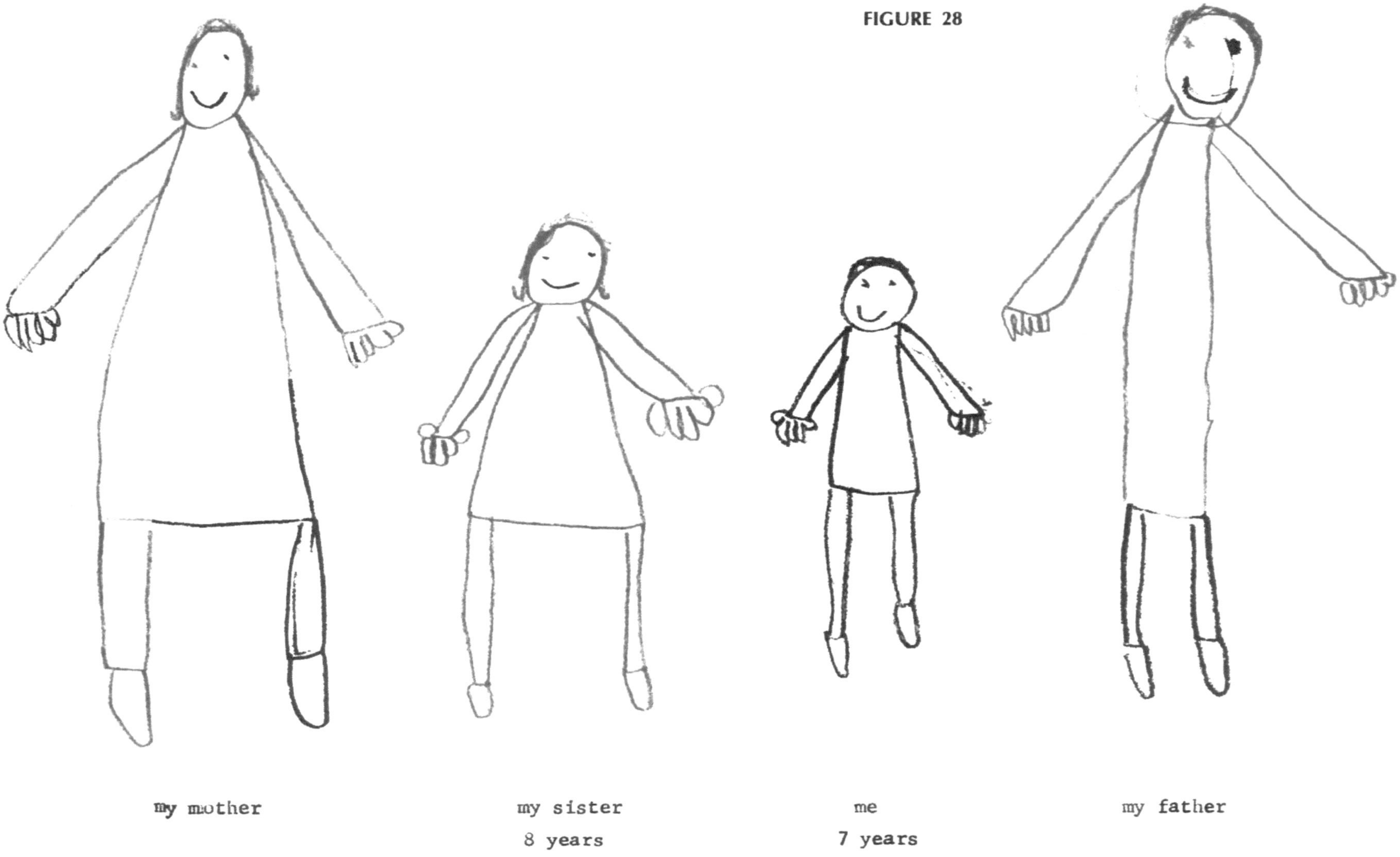

Disability portrayed in a self-drawing

The degree of verism necessary to portray a disability in a self-drawing is not to be expected until the child is at least seven or eight years old. It is only when the transition has occurred from intellectual to visual realism (Luquet) or, in cognitive terms, from the preoperational to the concrete operations stage (Piaget), that drawings become increasingly objective.

The self-portrait by a hemiplegic child of six years, four months (Figure 29) is in advance of his chronological age but quite in conformity with his mental age, eight years. His WISC IQ is 127.

He has drawn the right side of the figure with smaller extremities, just as his own right side is smaller. He has a spastic hemiplegia that has impaired the growth of his limbs on the right, the result of damage to the left side of his brain. The ability to "cross-over" (to tell which is right and left of a person sitting opposite) is manifested in the child's correct portrayal of the affected limbs rather than the mirror image, as a child would do before the seven- or eight-year level of maturity.

FIGURE 29

Visual realism in drawing of self.

Chronological age: 6 yrs 4 mos. Mental age: 8 yrs. WISC IQ: 127 Child has a right hemiplegia with poorly developed, smaller right upper and lower extremities; right equinus, strabismus.

In the drawing, the right arm and leg are smaller. He has not drawn the mirror image of his right side but has crossed over.

The ability to do this is usually acquired at age 7-8.

FIGURE 29

FIGURE 30

This drawing by a Vietnamese refugee tells a good deal about him.

One of my more challenging and fascinating assignments at the New York Foundling Hospital has been the determination of foundling age.

I do not claim any unique powers of divination, only the cumulative experience of 31 years as director of the Developmental Clinic.

During the debacle in Vietnam, a young boy was found wandering the streets. He was brought to the USA as a refugee. Because of his small stature and malnourished state, he was thought to be about four years of age. It soon became apparent, however, that his abilities were well above that age level. Accordingly, he was referred to my clinic.

The boy was highly suspicious at first, sat down at a table facing me, but would not make a move. Verbal communication was out of the question, for he knew no English and I no Vietnamese. He was highly alert, "on guard," scanning me and the place. Slowly shedding his defenses, his expression became more relaxed and we began to exchange smiles. Eventually, feeling safer, he took the crayon and began to draw a human figure. Having finished it, he looked at me, pointed to my beard and added it to the figure.

It was obvious from the drawing, that I was not dealing with a four-year-old. Using the Goodenough-Harris scoring, I estimated the drawing to express a mental age of seven and a half years. Furthermore, the addition of the beard represented a touch of visual realism, a stage in drawing behavior that begins usually between 7 and 8.

And finally, the fact that he had drawn the limbs on the left side smaller than those on the right was evidence that he had achieved the concept of "crossing over," by which I mean the ability to know which is right and left of a person facing. In this case, the person facing him was his drawing, in which he correctly drew on the left side of the figure, his own small paralyzed left arm and leg, the sequelae of polio.

Curiously, he drew his own body, then, possibly with a view to totally disarming me by a gesture of friendship, he added my beard and mustache. (The figure, incidentally, is Oriental.)

On the basis of his drawing, and disregarding stature, head circumference, weight, and bone age—all extremely misleading in such a malnourished child—I estimated him to be between seven and eight years. Support to this view was provided by his drawing of a diamond (**Figure 31**). Copy of the diamond is expected at age seven.

Accordingly, having estimated his age as seven and one half, I assigned him a birthdate by figuring back from the date of the evaluation. It was eventually learned that he had been born sometime in 1968. I saw him in April of '75.

FIGURE 30

FIGURE 31

Copy of a diamond by Vietnamese refugee boy, April 1975.

14

CREATIVITY

Creativity has been defined as the rearrangement of preexisting forms, objects, and facts in a new order by the conceptual and emotional activity of the mind (Lansing, 1969). For Victor D'Amico (1973), "the essence of creativity is to find a new thing and use it in a new way." These definitions are two ways of expressing the same concept, since what preexists is new to the child. "In the art of children we are enabled to see again the world as it is on the first time around" (Barron, 1973).

The arts—music, dance, modeling, drawing, painting, drama, literature—offer a most valuable and enjoyable opportunity for expression of imagination, fantasy, emotions, and creativity. Among the arts, the visual arts provide a unique experience, for while the other art forms can be perceived only in a time sequence, the visual arts present their content simultaneously and totally. Form, color, and relationships make their impact at once.

And among the visual arts, drawing is especially well suited to the abilities of children, who because of their age or disability are better able to control a crayon than brush or clay. In drawing, figures are more easily contained and details more easily and clearly represented. The activity is most appealing to young children and can be presented free from outside influence or suggestion, allowing maximum freedom of expression. Of value to the interested adult—parent, teacher, or investigator—is the record of the child's experience for future reference and comparison with subsequent products.

In drawing, the preëxisting forms that can be rearranged in a new order are the lines, arcs, circles, and other configurations and geometric shapes that the child learns to use in a symbolic representation of reality. Preeminent among these shapes is the circle. It is within the circle that the child of three to four will visualize an object—probably a head. And that event will mark the transition from kinesthetic to representational drawing. Egocentricity will continue to dominate thought until seven or eight; accordingly, the drawings will reflect the subjective nature of thought, and will be more a statement about the child himself than about the object portrayed. They will combine realism and expressionism to show a reality that is more in the mind than in the object.

If the child is encouraged but not directed, he will express thought and feelings in a personal, creative way, in a way similar to but not identical with that of children who have reached the same developmental stage. All children go through the same stages but each child does the same thing in an individual way.

The actual model serves as a cue. Portrayal is an expression of an inner realism, of what has impressed the child and is present in awareness at the time the figure is drawn. But in addition to content, there tends to be an unconscious expression of underlying emotional elements evidenced in the manner, which may be free or overly cautious, bold or hesitant, the figure large or tiny, the pressure strong or light, the line continuous or broken.

The urge to create is universal. During the preschool years it is likely to be intense, expressing itself in thought, language, and activity; in initiative, imaginative play, and in fantasy; in role playing, music, dance, and in the visual arts. The drawings gradually become more elaborate, with addition of more parts and sex appropriate traits.

The creative spirit inherent in every child should find encouragement and free expression during these preschool years if it is to survive. The world is new and yet to be discovered. Vision is direct, fresh, and personal. The view is not "wrong"; it is simply different from the adult's. In many ways it is a truer vision that often penetrates into the core of things.

By age seven or eight, the child's drawings will reflect to an increasing degree the realism that is slowly permeating his thought, making him more like most of us, lacking in spontaneity, imagination, and creativity—unless the danger is recognized and something is done to check the pull towards stifling conformism.

Actual art training—if by that is meant teaching what to do and how to do it—is inadvisable. Particularly during the preschool years, it suffices to suggest to the group just a general topic, say "a parade," allowing each child to express the idea in complete freedom. The results will be original and quite varied. They should be approved, admired. Avoiding direct questions, the instructor should encourage the child to elaborate verbally. No correction or adverse criticism, judgment or unfavorable comparison should be made. At issue is not the aesthetic quality of the product but the child's creative effort.

The loss of spontaneity and creativity noted in many children during the school years has been attributed to the untimely introduction of so-called art training. However, is the teacher to be just a passive spectator for fear of curbing and destroying creativity? A distinction must be drawn between freedom to create and boundless, unconfined self-expression. Experience and art training are doubtless assets in the teacher. But sensitivity to the changing aspects of child behavior is an indispensable element if one is to know when and how far to intervene, and how to tell the difference between creative self-affirmation and uninhibited disorganization. Nature itself has built-in limitations to wasteful elaboration.

It is never too early to cultivate the aesthetic taste. Exposure to sounds, sights, sensation and motion that offer an aesthetic experience is necessary in order to mobilize the inherent potential that can elevate one above the level of the beast. The beast approaches a flower, smells it, and turns away if it is not edible. To the beast, a sunset is a time to retire or, for the mosquito, a time to wake up—nothing to admire. The beast exists in Everyman. The arts are a most valuable elevating force accessible to Man alone.

Training in the use of a variety of media is helpful in that it increases the child's ability to give expression to perceptions and ideas.

Copying the work of others undermines the child's will to create. Imitation of work by the masters is of value to the more mature, who are already firm in the freedom to act creatively. The widespread use of coloring books is deplorable. They do keep children busy and quiet. It is said that they help children to control their hands and fingers as the coloring is done within the figure. But why not have the child draw his own figure and color his own creation?

I may have been using the term *creativity* in too broad a sense. One might say that I have been applying it to making something that was not there before. A distinction needs to be drawn between the term as applied to the work of children and its use in the world of art and artists. In a more restricted sense, creativity is a process in which two stages can be identified: the first, an intuitive one associated with feelings of enthusiasm or exultation (some call it madness); then, a stage of execution of the inspiration. As one observes the children busily representing their concepts on paper, one is often struck by the enthusiasm, even exultation that accompanies their efforts. The first stage is there but the second stage is seriously hampered by their lack of skill in carrying out the inspiration. Therefore, if by creative is intended that which is not only original but also of positive aesthetic value, the art of children falls short of meeting these criteria.

Parallels continue to be drawn between the graphic activity of children and that of early man, such as has been discovered in the caves of Altamira and Lascaux. Children, too, like to draw animals. In both child and early man the vision is fresh, direct, and essential. But the work of children cannot possibly reflect the degree of aesthetic sense and skill of execution that are so strikingly expressed in the cave paintings. Such creativity is even far beyond the capacity of the vast majority of adults.

Appreciation of beauty

As humans, it is our privilege to experience delight in the presence of beauty, to be attracted by what is aesthetic and to be repelled by what is disorderly, monstrous, filthy. The aesthetic experience eludes definition. Something of its nature may be said to derive from the attractiveness of its constituent parts, but above all from their fitting relationship to one another and from their contribution to the general effect of the whole. A person may be endowed with lovely eyes and limbs, but if the other features appear as though borrowed from someone else, the total effect can hardly be aesthetic. The concept of beauty is not limited to what we see but applies to all forms of sensory and motor organization: sound, touch, movement. Analysis is likely to destroy beauty; synthesis may produce it.

In an orchestra, each single player may be a master of his instrument, but if the individual elements do not relate suitably to one another and to the production of an integrated effect, it will be as though they were tuning up. The result would be anything but an aesthetic delight. The same synthesis applies to action. A beautiful woman, smartly gowned, does not offer an aesthetic experience if she is incongruously down on her knees scrubbing the floor. On the contrary, in Picasso's picture of a "Woman Ironing" every line, every item, every feature contributes to the general, strikingly touching effect of poverty, fatigue, and resignation to a hopeless fate.

The aesthetic sense is not inborn. It does not emerge fully armed as did Athena from the head of Zeus. The potential for its development is innate but it must be cultivated. This is a task for the family and the school.

Can the work of children be regarded as true art? This question is so charged with aesthetic and philosophical implications that I shall not even attempt an answer beyond saying that what children produce is *child art.* It is at once representational and expressive, intellectual and colored by feelings. Within technical limitations, it reveals the child's perception of a reality that is paradoxically unrealistic (by adult standards) and symbolic.

The creation of true works of visual art, such as we see in galleries, must await the maturation of intellect, emotions, aesthetic sense, and technical skill. Biographers of the master artists and sculptors, carried away by enthusiastic admiration for their heroes, have often told of marvelous early expressions of budding genius. Vasari tells how Leonardo as a boy drew some laughing women's faces that seemed to come from the hand of a master; how in his tender years, Filippo Lippi produced a marvelous painting for the Carmelites; how Giotto as a shepherd boy was surprised by Cimabue as he was drawing a lovely sheep on a slab, using a pointed stone, and how Cimabue, having taken Giotto into his studio, tried repeatedly to brush away with his hand a fly that the boy had painted on the nose of a face that the master had made. But where are these childhood masterpieces? They are nowhere to be seen. The fact is that greatness in the visual arts does not proclaim itself in childhood. The art work of children does not tell who among them will become tomorrow's Michelangelo or Picasso.

Training in visual arts in the Soviet Union

Training in the visual arts plays a prominent role in the education of Soviet children. "Aesthetic education" begins in the preschool but it is in the elementary school that actual training in the visual arts is carried out.

Despite divergences in specific programs—inevitable in a vast territory with a variety of cultural and ethnic groups—there is an overall philosophy to which all seem to defer: that the genuinely artistic work must represent as well as express. The element of objectivity and the artist's own subjective expression are regarded as characteristics of the artistic image. This view of aesthetics tends to emphasize the realistic aspect of art work. It is in sharp contrast with a viewpoint current in the Western world, that tends towards the abstract in art.

These divergences are reflected in the methods adopted in the training of children. In the Soviet Union, there is perhaps more emphasis on the technical use of media, on the development of technical skills. In many Western art classrooms, there prevails a permissiveness that might be considered excessive when paint is used as a vehicle for the expression of unbridled emotion. Representation, expression, and abstraction are all means by which master artists communicate their vision of life.

Despite the emphasis on art education, Soviet children show the same decline in creativity and interest in art work that has been noted among Western children as they approach adolescence.

Influences that tend to stifle the creative impulse

I should like to call attention to two nefarious influences that operate insidiously to sap the child's natural creative impulse. One is the widespread use of coloring books, of which I have already written. (For an extended discussion see my earlier book, *Young Children and Their Drawings,* 1970). The other negative influence is the trick of the stick man, by means of which the child is shown how to simplify the whole problem of drawing a person by reducing him to a circle and a few lines. By this device, even the most artistically inept are able to represent a person standing, sitting, walking, running, doing almost anything. Little wonder then that once we acquaint the child with this trick, he will likely adopt it in favor of his own personal rendition of the human figure at rest or in action.

Stick men, birds represented by two arcs joined at one end, and other stereotyped schemata, are found in workbooks aimed at teaching mathematical concepts. It is doubtful whether teaching number concepts by having the child color five schematized birds blue or red has any instructional value. However it does tend to influence the child's attempts at expressing his own internal model of a bird.

The case of the stick man

Do children naturally represent the trunk by a line or is this an artifact acquired from the adult?

To answer the question, I have examined drawings by preschool children in my own collection and those reproduced by investigators here and abroad. I have purposely chosen the younger children on the assumption that they are less likely to have succumbed to adult influences in their graphic activity. The drawings studied were made by children between the ages of three and six (Piaget's pre-operational stage). During this stage, children's drawings express an intellectual realism, an "internal model," a view that is still the child's own. Later on, the child will be influenced to see things "correctly."

The earliest publication with actual reproductions of drawings by children was a study by Corrado Ricci, a famous art critic, which appeared in Bologna in 1887. Ricci began collecting the drawings in 1883. There is not a single stick man in any of the drawings reproduced in Ricci's *L'Arte dei Bambini.* In each, the trunk is represented by a circular figure.

In 1905, *Kinderzeichnungen bis zum 14. Lebensjahr* was published in Leipzig. The author, Siegfried Levinstein, illustrated his work profusely with drawings by young children. In no instance is the trunk represented by a single line. In some, the trunk is a triangle or a square; in the vast majority it is a circular configuration. In none of the drawings reproduced in Florence Goodenough's (1926) *Measurement of Intelligence by Drawings* is there a stick man. Helda Eng (Norway), in her *Psychology of*

Children's Drawings (written in 1931) writes, "The body is at first only the open space between two lines which represent both body and legs; later on, it is marked off by a cross-stroke and also represented by an oval, a circle, or a rectangle; the attempt is finally made to make it more naturalistic." There are examples of "bodies drawn by beginners at the elementary school in Oslo"—none is a single line.

In his book, *"Entwicklungspsychologie des zeichnerischen Gestaltens"* (1955), Günther Mühle has included numerous examples of human figure drawings by young children. In none is the body a single line. There are no stick men. Nor are there any in the drawings reproduced in Dale B. Harris' *Children's Drawings as Measures of Intellectual Maturity* (1963), the single exception being a stick man drawn by a retarded girl of 12.

But just as I was about to make a general statement to the effect that the untutored child will never draw a stick man, I was startled to find, in my own collection, two instances in which very young artists, one a boy of 49 months, the other a girl of only 43 months, drew a human figure with a body represented by a single vertically oriented line. In view of the tender age of both these children, I find it difficult to believe that they had adopted the adult schema. Long ago, I learned that one should never say "never" or "always." However, are two children going to demolish the formidable mass of evidence that preschool children *almost invariably* represent the trunk in circular form? As for myself, I remain in full agreement with D.G. Kerschensteiner's statement (1905) that young children do not draw stick men, that they do not draw a trunk consisting of a single line (those two rascals notwithstanding).

These following drawings illustrate early ways of representing the trunk. **Figure 32** by a boy of four years, seven months is especially interesting because of the original treatment of the eyes. He explained that it is a self-portrait and that he is asleep and awake. Hence the four eyes, two closed and two open wide. He is a very active, sociable child. The figure has many fingers with which to enter into contact with his environment and 9 legs with which to move about. In these drawings the trunk, as in the overwhelming majority of drawings by preschool children, is represented two-dimensionally.

FIGURE 32

FIGURE 33

Drawing by a girl of five years 10 months.

FIGURE 34
Drawn by a boy age six years, eight months.

FIGURE 35

Drawn by boy of seven years, seven months. Stanford-Binet IQ 100.

FIGURE 36

Exception to the rule. Stick man drawn by girl age 43 months.

The stick man is often seen in drawings by school age children. What are the influences that cause children to adopt this schematic figure? The stick man, an oversimplified schema of the human body, is seen by children in workbooks and in some misguided interventions by adults who think they are teaching the child how to draw. The stick man is commonly used by adults to portray movement. Many children are quick to grasp the ease with which the stick figure can save them the trouble of trying to draw a satisfactory trunk. The phenomenon of inertia prevails and the development of human figure drawing comes to a halt.

A few drawings by school age children (Figure 37, 38, and 39) make the point quite clearly. The child, seduced by an adult visual cliché, is unlikely to continue to develop artistically.

FIGURE 37

Stick man drawn by a boy of six who has just finished kindergarten.

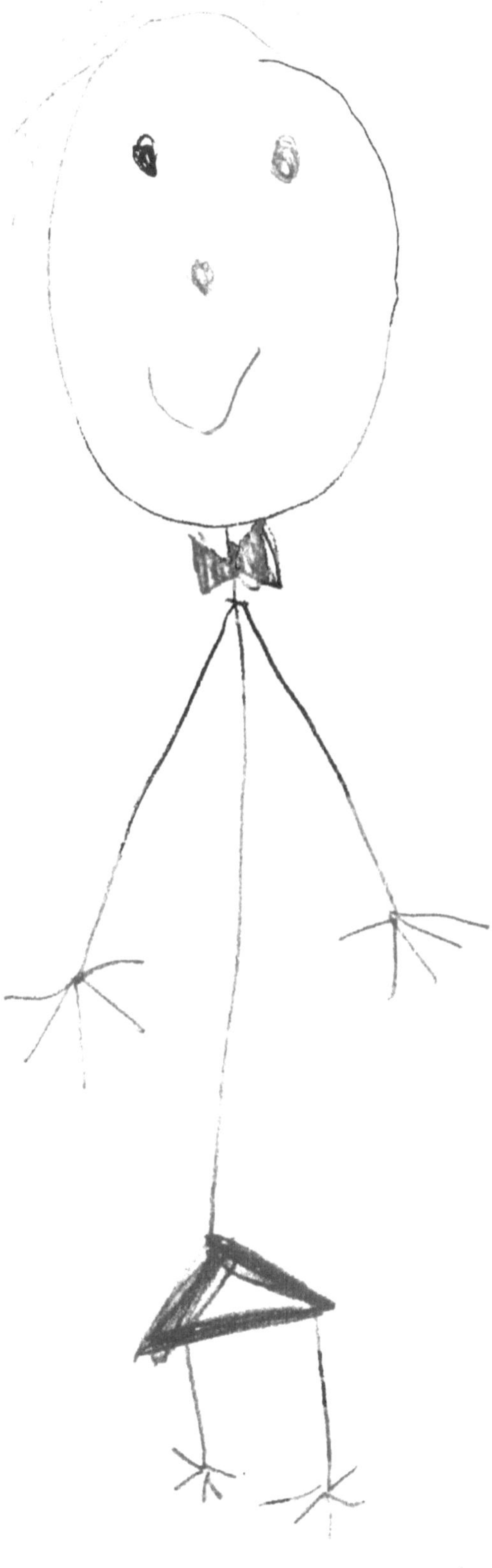

FIGURE 38

Drawn by a boy ten years, nine months.

FIGURE 39

Ten years, nine months.

FIGURE 40

Drawn by boy of eight years, 10 months. Doing well in third grade.

Examiner: "Draw a person walking."
Child: "Can I make him running?"
Examiner: "Fine, go ahead."

The child, faced with the difficulty of portraying action, is likely to adopt this:

as an easy way out if given encouragement.

15

CHILD ART AS A UNIFYING PRINCIPLE

In the evolution of pictorial forms, a pivotal moment is the child's discovery that a casually drawn circle may become a symbolic representation of an object perceived. This event, at the threshold of representational art, is a quantum leap from the preceding level of kinesthetic scribbling. Its universality extends beyond the world of children; the circular form is found everywhere that visual symbols were and are being made. The discovery and use of the circle as a basic image are independent of racial, cultural, or individual variables, for it is rooted in the very structure and function of the nervous system. This system sets the ways in which all of us can sense, perceive, think, understand, and act. It manifests the fundamental unity of mankind.

In its universality, Jung saw the circular configuration as an archetype, as part of the collective unconscious. The circle, modified by addition and elaboration, will serve to express concept and emotion. But underlying all creativity is the nervous system which provides the sensori-motor function and eye-hand coordination that make the circle possible mechanically. Over and above those functions is that of marshalling the sensory input into meaningful arrangement or patterns, thereby bringing order out of chaos, preparing the way for logical thought. The universality of the image in its form and in its message, in time and in space, in its communicability, and in its capacity for aesthetic development makes it a powerful unifying principle in the midst of so much that divides and disturbs.

The arts unite people. Better than any international language, the arts speak a universal language, the language of mind and emotions. Music, dance, literature and drama are all powerful influences for the aesthetic enrichment of life and for creative expression. The development of aesthetic taste should begin early if it is to abide and add pleasure and meaning to life.

Child art, in cutting across barriers of time and space and cultures, has been aptly called "a visual Esperanto." The universality of the child's pictorial symbols, as manifested in spontaneous drawings, is but another affirmation of the oneness of mankind. Cultivation of the languge of symbols merits a central position in the education of the young, and especially so during the early years when the will to create and to express one's thoughts and feelings is intense and still unfettered.

It is not enough to expose children to good art. They will have to make art if they are to benefit. Little encouragement is needed, for these activities are eagerly entered into and thoroughly enjoyed.

Through graphic activity and modeling, the children express the changes that occur in their perception of reality as they assimilate and organize sense impressions in their progress from stage to stage. At the same time, they are communicating, unknowingly, feelings that they cannot or will not verbalize. The concepts and emotions expressed graphically may not provide the viewer with an aesthetic experience, but the expression is a very personal one and is often delightful and informative.

Lacking technical skill and a deep vision of life, the child cannot be expected to produce works that meet the aesthetic and intellectual criteria by which a work is judged as having artistic merit. The widespread interest and fascination with the works of children must lie elsewhere. Berthold Lowenfeld feels that their universal appeal resides not in their being products of art but in their being products of children.

One has but to attend a concert, a ballet, an opera, an exhibition of paintings to witness the universal appeal of all the arts: young and old, white, black, and Oriental, conservative and radical, all pay homage by their attendance and appreciation to the genius of those who have labored and struggled to provide the rich heritage, a most valuable relic of the past. Art is indeed a unifying principle. Sir Herbert Read (1966) with abundant good reason looks upon education through art as education for peace.

The child's creative urge may cause him to embark on projects that express initiative and imagination but that are obviously of impossible realization. At issue is the freedom to think one's own thoughts, to discover the enthralling world, to seek the unfamiliar, and to act creatively. Imposition of adult standards, discouraging comments, and failure to express appreciation and praise will tend to extinguish the creative flame in all but the most determined or the highly talented. The history of art is replete with instances of those who successfully fought off the forces of conformism and went on to create the works that are the delight and treasure of civilized man. But such gifts and clarity of mission are not widely dispensed.

PART THREE

Synthesis

16

A DEVELOPMENTAL PERSPECTIVE

Behavior can be understood and appraised only in terms of what has gone before and what is coming. The present is but a moment in a dynamism that stems from the past and hearkens to the future. The child is not a miniature adult. Physically, as well as functionally, the child is not only quantitatively, but above all, qualitatively, different. What is normal in the child may be quite abnormal in the adult. One may say that all this is obvious, were it not for the fact that errors and judgments based on adult standards are widespread and persistent. Probably, underneath the fallacy is a notion that the child is a defective adult.

It may not be superfluous to remind ourselves of certain important differences between child and adult functioning, other than the obvious physical ones.

The incoordination that characterizes the fumbling grasping by the five-month-old would suggest cerebellar dysfunction in an older person, as would the staggering gait of the child just past the first birthday.

An important item in a neurological examination is the Babinski reflex. In stroking the outer border of the foot, the great toe dorsiflexes, pointing, as it were, an accusing finger at the brain. And indeed, in the older child and adult the Babinski reflex is a sign of damage to the brain or to the upper motor neuron. But in an infant, this reflex simply tells us that the cerebral cortex has not as yet extended its controlling influence over the muscles of the foot. It is quite normal for that age level.

An electroencephalogram showing an alpha-type activity of seven cycles per second would be well within normal range for a child of five years but not so if the child were 12.

Inability to copy a diamond at 10 would raise the question of possible retardation or perceptual impairment, whereas the same difficulty would be the norm before age seven.

The undeveloped body-image differentiation that characterizes the normal symbiosis of an infant would indicate arrest in ego development were it to persist in an older child.

In evaluating and interpreting children's drawings, the application of adult criteria often leads to invalid statements of abnormality. Items such as an excessive number of fingers or long sticks for fingers, when they occur in drawings by adults, are interpreted as symbolic of acquisitiveness or aggression. But in drawings by preschool children stick fingers are the rule, and they are often either too many or too few.

Figure 41 by a bright, well-adjusted girl of only four years, seven months has supernumerary digits. The drawing, incidentally, expresses high level intelligence.

Figure 42 by a bright, well-adjusted girl of five years, three months, shows a person with only three fingers and toes for each extremity.

But Figure 43 by a boy of five years, six months, a self-portrait (he said "it's me"), is characterized by large arms, excessive number of very long spiky fingers, and huge teeth. This boy is bright, but quite hostile and aggressive. The drawing, taken as a whole, conveys his reaction to rejection by his mother, his father having long since vanished. The boy is living in an institution pending placement in foster care.

FIGURE 41

In this drawing by a bright, well adjusted girl of four years, seven months we see the long spiky fingers that are typically seen in drawings by young children. The correct number of fingers is not expected in drawings by preschool children. After all, representing fingers by sticks is by far the simplest way of handling of very difficult problem. Spiky fingers at this age level may not be symbolic of emotional disorder.

FIGURE 42

This human figure by a girl of five years, three months is at a fully average level for her chronological age. There is nothing abnormal about the fact that there are only three digits per limb. Preschool children typically draw the wrong number of fingers and toes and, also typically, they represent them by sticks.

FIGURE 43

Hostility and aggression are expressed in this drawing by a boy of five years, eight months. He is reacting to rejection by his parents. As a whole and in its parts, this drawing tells how he feels. Huge teeth, long spiky fingers.

In young children, caution is recommended in attaching symbolic value to items that may be of developmental rather than pathognomonic significance. The total impression conveyed by the drawing is usually more valid than focus on specific items. Of the three drawings, the one by the boy, taken in toto, is suggestive of hostility and aggression, and so are its parts. But the whole is always greater than the sum of its parts.

Whatever its significance in drawings by adults or older children, a disproportionately large head is a typical feature of drawings by young children and simply expresses the primacy of the head in the child's concept of the body image (see Figures 44,45,46, and 47).

The same developmental perspective is essential as regards the disproportionately small trunk, also a common feature in drawings by young children, who thereby express the secondary importance which they attach to one's trunk. (For a fuller discussion of these and other peculiarities the reader is referred to *Young Children and Their Drawings,* Di Leo, 1970).

Large eyes (see Figures 45 and 46) may symbolize a suspicious attitude in adult drawings, but this is not so in drawings by young children. Enormous heads and eyes like goggles are typically seen in early representations of the human body. "For a long time the head will continue to dominate the figure as it does in the living person. . . .The head will promptly be fitted with conspicuous eyes. . . . . .Even in earliest infancy, nothing will engage the baby's attention like the human face; but within the face it is the eyes that spellbind as activity subsides" (Di Leo, 1970).

FIGURE 44

Universality of large head and small trunk in drawings of young children.

FIGURE 45

Human figure drawing by girl of four years, nine months, expresses better than average concept of body image.

FIGURE 46

Drawn by a boy of four years, two months. A human figure without arms is often seen in drawings by four- and five-year-olds, and should not be considered abnormal.

FIGURE 47

In this drawing by a boy of six years, 10 months, the absence of arms is related to some of his personality traits. He is overly cautious, non-aggressive, does not like "rough" children. He bites his nails. He was asked to draw a person and produced this drawing of a female, quite at variance with what the majority of boys his age would do.

Omission of the upper extremities is atypical at his age.

The symbolism of the tree

Among the drawing tests used to assess personality, the drawing of a tree is regarded as especially revealing of the individual's relationship to the environment (Buck, 1948). Apart from its assumed significance as a universal archetype, the tree probably offers a vehicle for the freer expression of an adult's deeper feelings than does the human figure drawing. The subject is said to be less likely to feel threatened and consequently less inclined to mobilize defenses than in the more obvious personal situation of drawing the human figure.

Here, again, the developmental perspective is essential lest we attribute significance to what might be "pathoformic" when drawn by the adult, but quite usual in the drawings of children.

Eventually children emphasize the trunk, a feature that has an entirely different significance than the ego strength attributed to an impressive trunk when it appears in adult drawings.

I have often seen trees without roots drawn by adults who actually had no roots in the social world. But when children draw trees without roots they are doing what most children do.

Trees bearing fruits are said to symbolize children, or the desire to have them. I hesitate to attribute the same significance to the apples that I have often seen hanging from the child's tree.

A knot-hole or a scar in the adult's tree may symbolize a traumatic or emotionally memorable experience. Its location on the trunk may indicate the time when the event occurred. This is determined by measuring the tree and locating the scar along the presumed life-line as represented by the height of the tree. I am not convinced that this interpretation applies to knot-holes in children's trees. I must, however, mention the report by Toker (1971) of a seven-year-old girl who drew a tree with a hole in the trunk suggestively symbolic of the hole in her heart. She was to undergo surgery for repair of an atrial septal defect.

In general, the drawing viewed as a whole is more revealing than attempts to attach a point-by-point significance to specific items.

A century of studies of children's drawings here and abroad confirms the child's preference for the human body as subject. While it is true that adults are less likely to summon defenses when asked to draw a tree rather than a human figure—as they are probably not aware that the tree is interpreted as a symbol of themselves—the same does not hold for children. Children are more likely to inhibit and censor their verbal utterances than they are to detect invasion of privacy in their spontaneous drawings or in their compliance with a request to draw a person.

I am convinced that, so far as children are concerned, human figures tell us a great deal more than their trees. Exception may be made for those children who have become excessively self-conscious because of a handicapping condition. These children may tend to project their anxiety to the tree or some object less clearly symbolic of themselves than the human figure.

FIGURE 48

A boy of 10 has drawn "a boy" (himself) between two trees. He is living in a residential facility away from his parents who have separated and are unable to provide a home. He attends an ungraded class. I believe the two trees symbolize his parents. He has added a bird overhead and a fish in water.

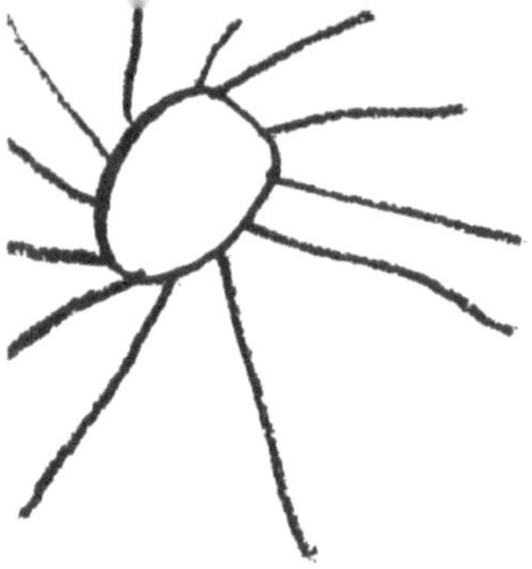

FIGURE 49

Drawn by a girl of seven and a half years. School phobia. She vomits before school but not on weekends. The smaller child is her younger sister. The apple tree has a large trunk, darkened by vertical lines. She is on the side away from the sun. The shading of the trunk is interpreted as expressive of anxiety. The scene indicates a preference for the outdoors.

FIGURE 48

FIGURE 50

There is a knot-hole in the impressive trunk drawn by this girl of seven. In her history, there is no known unusual physical or emotional traumatic event. The mood in this idyllic scene is peaceful and happy. She has picked a flower, the sun is shining, a bird is singing and other (schematized) birds are flying overhead, while a squirrel is climbing the trunk. The general impression conveyed is pleasant. Viewing the drawing as a whole is generally more informative than focusing on specific details, such as the knot-hole. Adult influence can be seen in the schematized birds.

FIGURE 51

Overemphasis of the trunk is quite common in young children. But this boy is 11 years of age. He presents with no behavioral problem at home and is well-behaved at school. The large trunk and the apples suggest immaturity, especially notable in the small, armless human figure beside the overwhelming tree. The human figure indicates intellectual limitations and passivity as well as feelings of inferiority. School performance is fair in fifth grade.

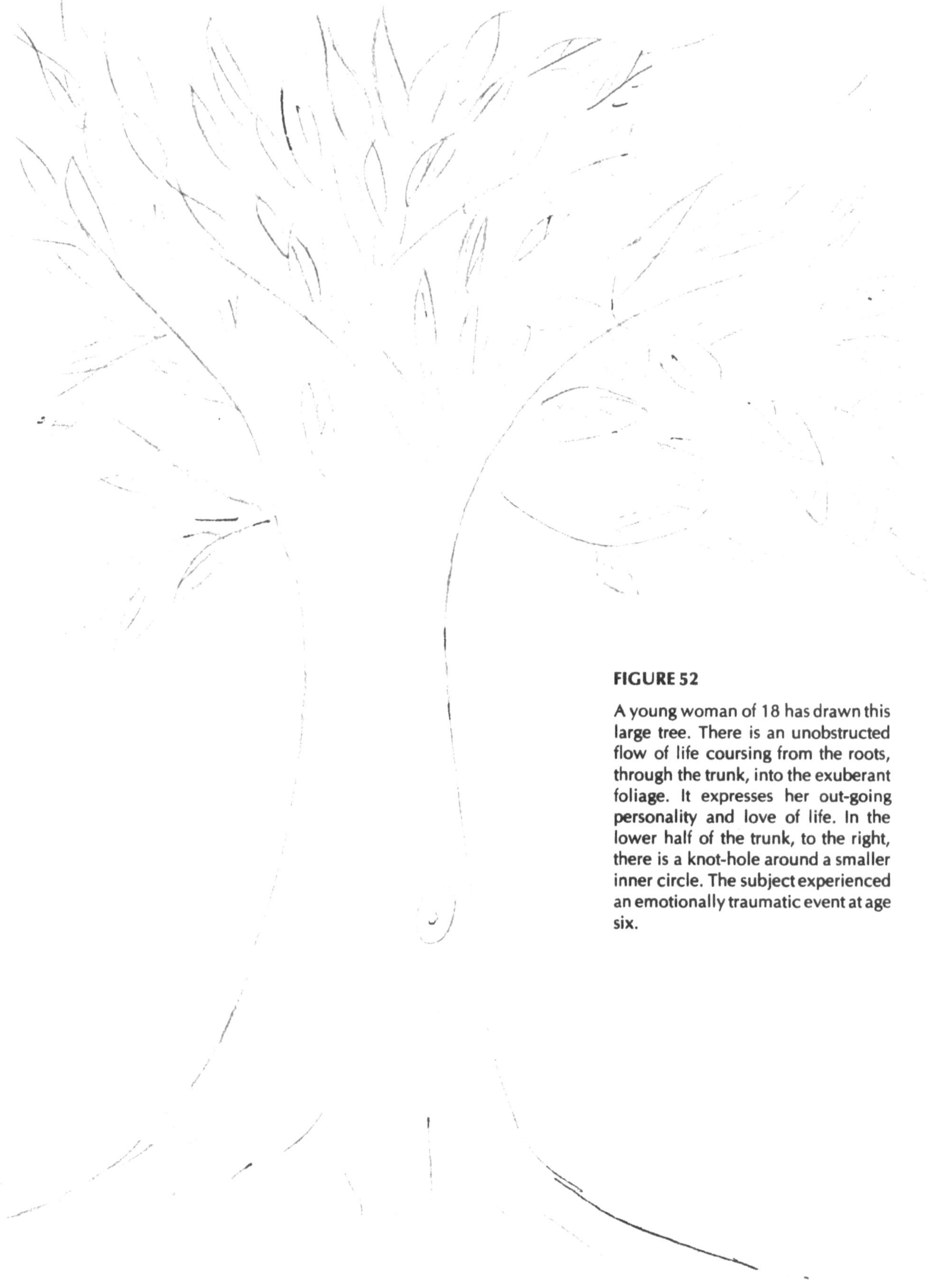

FIGURE 52

A young woman of 18 has drawn this large tree. There is an unobstructed flow of life coursing from the roots, through the trunk, into the exuberant foliage. It expresses her out-going personality and love of life. In the lower half of the trunk, to the right, there is a knot-hole around a smaller inner circle. The subject experienced an emotionally traumatic event at age six.

FIGURE 53

This tree, by a depressed young woman of 25, has a firmly outlined trunk, a feature that is regarded as indicating an emotionally dominated personality, (emphasis on the trunk is quite common in children's trees). The heavy shading suggests anxiety; the large hole and its location, a traumatic event during childhood. The absence of leaves and the circle of blades of grass that circumscribes the tree suggest isolation. She was a foster child, abandoned by her natural mother. Because of abusive behavior towards her three out-of-wedlock children, she is receiving social, educational, and psychological help. She is cooperating in a program of habilitation.

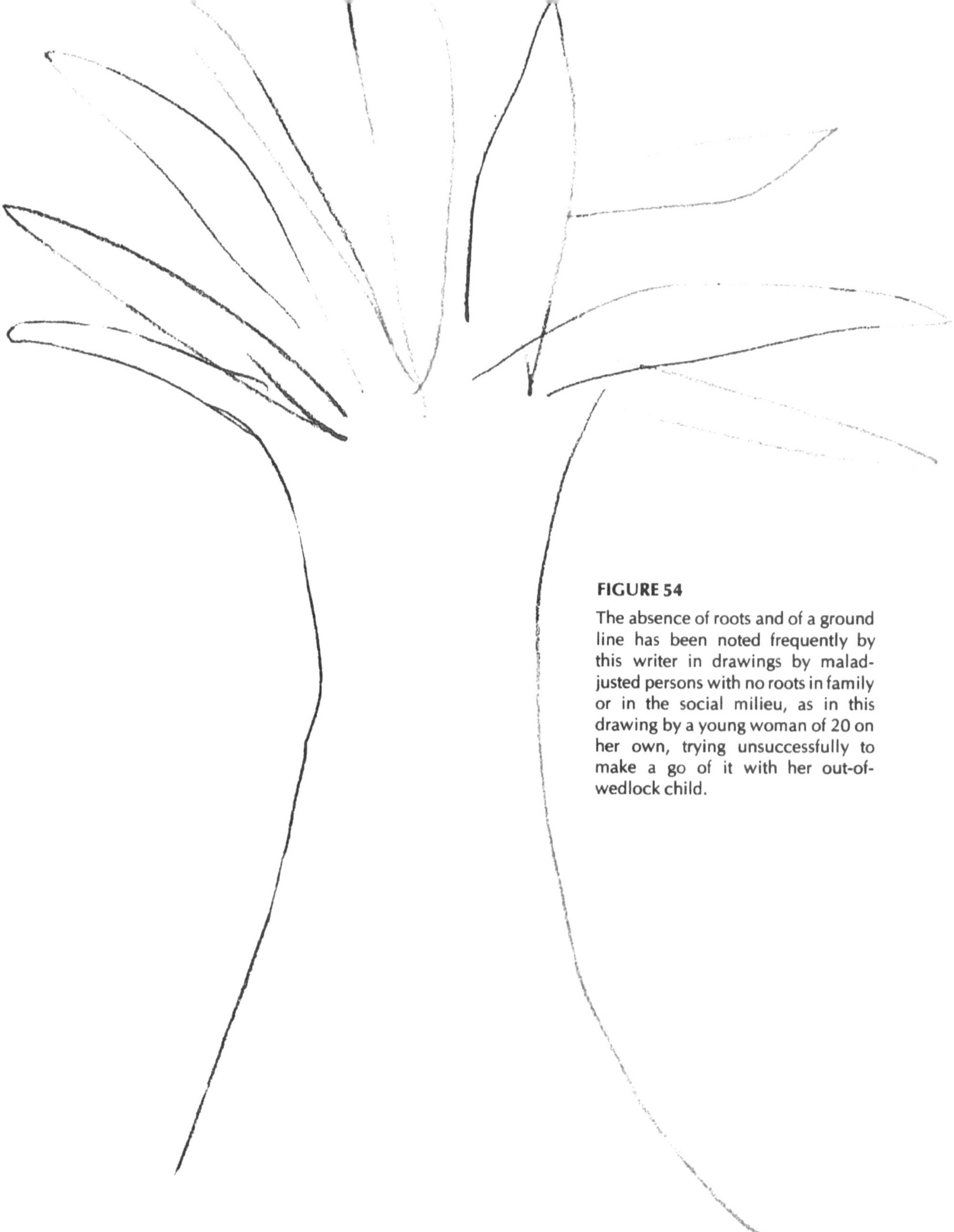

FIGURE 54

The absence of roots and of a ground line has been noted frequently by this writer in drawings by maladjusted persons with no roots in family or in the social milieu, as in this drawing by a young woman of 20 on her own, trying unsuccessfully to make a go of it with her out-of-wedlock child.

17

INTEGRATION: CORRELATIONS AND RELATIONSHIPS

The following episode in the early growth of language offers an excellent illustration of how all aspects of development interweave to form an indivisible unity.

The first clear labial consonant is heard at about six to seven months of age, when the infant begins to cry from a closed mouth and produces the sound "m-m-m." Prior to that time, the mouth was consistently open during crying so that such a sound could not be formed.

Setting aside the sound for a moment, and viewing it only as movement, it becomes evident that the movement of the lips is identical with that of sucking. In many languages, the Romance languages in particular, the sound produced by this movement of the lips has given rise to the word that denotes the female breast (mammella (Italian); mama (Spanish); mamelle (French)). Just as the infant begins with loving the food and other creature comforts and eventually transfers the libidinal drive onto the person in whose context the good things arrive, so does the term find its way from the immediate source of food to the giver (mamma, mama, maman, mutter, mother). An initially meaningless sound "m-m-m" has become the verbal symbol for the libidinal object.

Eventually, language is destined to assume a major role in the growth of cognition as well as in the expression of feelings.

Movement, sense, psychosexual and psychosocial developments combine and interact with each other and with language and cognition to form the unity that we call the *personality*.

Among the various approaches to child development there is a consensus regarding the existence of a period, roughly the first six months of life, when the infant provides no clear sign of awareness of a distinction between self and the environment.

This phenomenon is interpreted according to the observer's theoretical framework and is expressed in a terminology peculiar to that view.

Psychoanalysis stresses the importance of the physical and affective relationship in the development of individuation, conceived as a manifestation of the emergent ego, the establishment of object relations, and termination of the normal symbiotic condition.

Gesell views the development of a clear distinction between self and other persons in maturational terms fundamentally determined by intrinsic growth factors, contingent upon environment, and subject to individual variations.

Piaget speaks of adualism to express the lack of awareness of the external world as distinct from the organism, dualism being a state of knowing and being between the "me" and the "not me" (Kant). The two possess a separate, interacting reality. According to this theory, the young infant, at the beginning of psychic development, senses the environment in terms of his own actions, as a fleeting series of impressions, without stability or organization. The infant is unaware of the dualism that separates him from an outer world that has permanence and substance.

Psychoanalytic theory interprets the same phenomenon as infantile narcissism; there is no differentiation of "me" and "not me," and objects are "merely instinct-representations, lacking stability, and depending on the fluctuating satiation of the instinctual drive" (Rapaport, 1951).

Achievement of the concept of "I" and "Not I" has crucial implications for the development of ego functions. This concept of individuation offers an additional illustration of how the various aspects converge, integrate, and contribute to its formation.

Concurrently, as motor abilities mature, the toddler moves away from mother, while the budding ego is making him aware that his thoughts and desires may not coincide with the mother's, that they may even clash. At the same time, expressive language has been developing to a level that can give verbal notification of the physical, emotional, and cognitive separation that marks the end of the symbiotic phase. And scribbling leaves its individual, assertive markings for all to see.

Underlying all is the structural and functional maturation of the brain and neuromuscular apparatus.

18

A SYNOPTIC VIEW OF CHILD DEVELOPMENT

In preparing this chart, an effort was made to select significant items in each of the stages while abiding within limits that would allow a comprehensive view of the field. This procedure was beset with frequent and persistent doubt as to what to include or omit. To alleviate the uneasiness arising from such difficult and inescapable decisions, I have added an appendix in which the reader may find, in tabular form, a fuller summary of the characteristic features of the several aspects of child development.

The same spectacle of child development is viewed from different perspectives, giving rise to a variety of perceptions from which are derived hypotheses that are expressed in distinct linguistic terms. Yet within the diversity there is more that unites than divides. The device of a synoptic chart is an attempt to present a global view in the hope that similarities will overshadow the differences.

THE STAGES IN CHILD DEVELOPMENT – A SYNOPTIC CHART

APPROXIMATE AGE	MOTOR	PSYCHOSEXUAL	PSYCHOSOCIAL
0-1	PHYLOGENETIC REFLEXES Moro, tonic-neck, rooting, sucking, hand and toe grasp, stepping Babinski. Voluntary movements appear as cortical control spreads down the neural axis and out into the limbs: over eyes, mouth, arms, trunk, hands, fingers, legs, feet. Crawls, creeps, stands, walks.	ORAL symbiosis: 0-6 months sucking incorporation objectal phase: 6 months + discriminates stranger biting oral aggression	BASIC TRUST receiving and taking-in; mother/infant unity and interaction; constancy and consistency of mothering; mutually gratifying relationship.
1-2	LOCOMOTION AND GRASP precise pincer grasp; walks alone (12-15 months); runs, climbs (18 months);	distinction between I and NOT I; libidinal/aggressive drives fuse in object.	SEPARATION/ INDIVIDUATION awareness of self as separate from mother.
2-3	up and down stairs, jumps off floor, later off a step; pedals and steers tricycle; stands momentarily on one foot; builds towers of 9 cubes by age 3. Delights in scribbling.	ANAL retention/elimination ambivalence; resistance to habit training; strong motor drive.	AUTONOMY, Sense of muscular maturation; holding on/letting go; contradictory tendencies.
3-4	achieving effortless mastery over fine and gross motor activity; motor drive is intense. broad jump; stands on one foot several seconds;	PHALLIC assumes sex role; genitalia strongly cathected; female: receptive and inclusive; male: intrusive, verbal and physical attack;	INITIATIVE, Sense of the action system, now under control, is valued for what it can do; sex role established;
4-7	improved eye-hand coordination: draws circle and cross, eventually copies square, triangle and at age 7 a diamond. Uses scissors.	ambivalence towards parent of same sex Oedipus/Electra complex: frustration, guilt.	curiosity, fantasy, vivid imagination, creativity; conscience being formed; cooperates with peers in making and planning.
7-12	highly active: ball-play, riding bicycle, jump rope, swimming; uses knife, hammer; enjoys drawing, a fine means of self-expression; active participation in games with peers; tends to play to exhaustion.	LATENCY dynamics relatively stabilized; social adaptation to peers of same sex; gradual shift from narcissism to altruism; libido diverted to social ends.	INDUSTRY the wish and will to learn, applies self to tasks and to acquisition of skills; likes to produce things; satisfactions found in peer relationships; less involved with family.
Through the 'teens	May improve skill in sports or may prefer to watch; may over-extend self in competitive sports; may feel lacking in energy; need to overcome awkwardness due to rapid growth.	PUBERTY AND ADOLESCENCE gradual transfer of psychic energy to other sex, as influenced by Oepipus/ Electra complex; object cathexis: ideas, career.	IDENTITY, Search for Ideological. Who am I? Where do I belong? How do I appear to others? Clannish; over-identification with ideals of cliques and crowds. Need for approval and appreciation.
Main Sources	A. Gesell and co-workers	S. Freud A. Freud M. Mahler R. Spitz	E.H. Erikson

THE STAGES IN CHILD DEVELOPMENT – A SYNOPTIC CHART

COGNITIVE	LANGUAGE	DRAWING	ELECTRO-ENCEPHALO-GRAM	APPROX-IMATE AGE
<u>SENSORI-MOTOR</u> Reflexive: gradual development of goal-directed, purposeful behavior; thinks motorically;	<u>PRE-LINGUISTIC</u> Birth cry, throaty sounds, vowels, babbling, lallation, da-da, ma-ma playful sounds, Inner Language: claps hands on request, waves bye-bye. First word or two at end of first year; incipient jargon.	Crayon to mouth; does not draw.	no rhythmic activity during first 3 months After 3 months, first appearance of alpha-type waves and first appearance of clear voluntary movements as eyes follow moving object.	0-1
concept of object permanence; imitates; expressive language.	<u>EXPRESSIVE LANGUAGE</u> Single words, later 2-3 word combinations; abandons jargon and uses short sentences by end of second year. Uses pronouns I, me, you, mine, assertively and possessively. Speech reflects egocentricity: frequent monologues, affirmations, no account taken of other's position. Tells sex; uses plurals; rapidly expanding vocabulary; identifies and names colors; defines in terms of use; asks meaning of words; creates sentences he has never heard; many questions why, how. Articulation distinct. Learns to read and write.	<u>KINESTHETIC DRAWING</u> (scribbling) Crayon held in fist makes zig-zags; later a variety of configurations: whorls, eventually distinct circles; enjoys watching a record of motion on the paper; crayon will be guided by index finger.	alpha-type waves gradually increasing in frequency; now about 5 c.p.s.	1-2
<u>PRE-OPERATIONAL</u> (pre-conceptual phase 2 - 4 years) egocentric, subjective notion of cause-effect; beginning symbolic thought; classifies by form, color, later by size; increasing role of language.			child walks alone and plucks adeptly between index and thumb (exclusively human skill)	2-3
		<u>DISCOVERY</u> that the circle may serve to represent something, probably a head; has made a first graphic symbol.	alpha-type waves now about 8 c.p.s. child is achieving mastery over motor system	3-4
(intuitive phase 4 - 7 years) increased symbolic thought; still subjective but sees relationships; thinks in terms of classes; handles number concepts; focuses on only one trait at a time. Gradually decreasing domination of thought by perception.		<u>REPRESENTATIONAL DRAWING</u> <u>Expressionistic:</u> Subjective rendition of favorite theme: human body. <u>Intellectual Realism:</u> what is known to exist shall be shown; importance is expressed by size.		4-7
<u>CONCRETE OPERATIONS</u> less egocentric; concepts of conservation of quantity and weight; able to arrange items in series; can reverse in math; beginning to organize conceptually not just on basis of concrete aspects. Less dependent upon perceptual field.	Egocentricity diminishes and speech becomes increasingly a vehicle for exchange of opinions and ideas. Language interacts with thought in the elaboration of concepts.	<u>Visual Realism:</u> tries objective portrayal; body proportions more realistic, head no longer dominates figure; notion of visual perspective; profile tends to replace full-face orientation.	alpha activity elevated, about 11 c.p.s. as biological pre-puberal changes occur	7-12
<u>FORMAL OPERATIONS</u> abstract thought and conceptualization; truly logical; makes inferences; inductive and deductive reasoning; able to handle many variables at one time; makes and evaluates hypotheses.	Preoccupation with self may result in periods of silence, meditation. Many tend to argue and debate. Challenges any position taken by parents. At peak of psychomotor efficiency. Thinks and expresses highly abstract views.	<u>CRITICAL SENSE DEVELOPS</u> most tend to lose interest in expressing themselves in visual arts. Those who feel they are gifted will persevere; others will turn to other fields for self-expression and creative effort.	adult pattern is established: about 10 c.p.s.	**Through the 'teens**
J. Piaget	**R. Brown** **D. McCarthy** **H.R. Myklebust**	**C. Rucci** **G.H. Luquet** **J. Di Leo**	**D.B. Lindsley**	**Main Sources**

Epilogue

In any analysis of development into its component aspects, there will be considerable overlap. This is unavoidable. The motor is invaded by the emotional, and this by the cognitive and the perceptual, and all to an increasing degree by language and social factors. The interaction is complex, intimate, and reciprocal.

In attempting a synthesis, I have adopted a synoptic device rather than a discursive presentation. In my choice, I have been influenced by the visual arts. Unique among the arts, and, indeed, among all other forms of communication, they offer all their conceptual and emotional content immediately, at once. My intent has been to present a collection of the most coherent stage-dependent theories, to relate them to each other, as well as to experimentally documented behavior, and finally to offer the whole clinical spectacle synoptically. Imperfect as it may be, it is intended as a practical aid in keeping before us the unity and reality of the Child.

At appropriate intervals throughout the text, I have inserted drawings in the hope that these may vivify as well as illustrate the topics under consideration. My long fascination with the graphic products of the young has added immeasurably to my understanding of what Despert has sensitively called "the inner voices of children."

Beyond analysis

Somewhere between intellect and affect, there is a third faculty capable of acting upon perceptual material, and that is intuition. It defies measurement and logic—but so does the unconscious. Yet, there is wide acceptance of the role played by both intuition and the unconscious in human behavior.

Intuition is elusive, uncontrollable, appearing when least expected, often to reveal immediately and directly the core of a problem that may be inaccessible to methodical thought. It operates in all fields of human endeavor, in the sciences as well as in the arts. It may shed a clarifying light on the complexities and capriciousness of behavior, when statistical anaylsis yields impressive but only piecemeal or inconclusive data.

In our work with children and their parents, we are continually confronted with problems that call for understanding, assistance, and even crisis intervention. Were we to discard all knowledge that is not scientifically demonstrable by controlled, replicable experiment, there would remain precious little to offer those who turn to us for help. Research in child development is making highly significant contributions to our store of factual knowledge. Theories and intuitions are being tested and scrutinized; some are supported, others challenged. That is as it should be. In the meantime, which may be forever, we shall continue to invoke theory and intuition to fill the narrowing but enormous gap that eludes analysis and quantification.

The individualized, clinical approach remains the most fruitful diagnostically and the most effective therapeutically.

Appendix

INDIVIDUAL ASPECTS OF CHILD BEHAVIOR IN OUTLINE

Some aspects of progressive neural organization

age	
0–3 months	Behavior mediated from the midbrain. Phylogenetic reflexes: rooting, sucking, Moro, reflex hand and toe grasp. Sensory tracts myelinated and functioning (touch, pain, response to light and sound). Motor tracts from cortex unmyelinated, not functional. Electroencephalographic record disorganized, no rhythmic activity.
3 months +	Evidence of encephalization of behavior as control from the cortex begins to manifest itself in a cephalocaudad direction, i.e., down from the head and out into the limbs. The first sign of voluntary, cortically-controlled activity consists in conjugate movement of the eyes in pursuit of a moving object. This first clear sign from the cortex is associated with the appearance of rhythmic alpha-type activity in the EEG record. These waves are of low frequency about 3 cycles per second (c.p.s.) and are obtained from the occipital lobe in which the visual area is located.
12 months to 15 months	Cortical controls have been spreading downward as the cortico-spinal tracts are acquiring their myelin sheath. The child is now in good control of hands and can pluck precisely between index and thumb (pincer grasp) while at the same time he has achieved bipedal locomotion, unsteady at first with fewer returns to creeping as time goes on. Alpha-type waves are gradually increasing in frequency, now about 5 c.p.s.
3 years	Considerable mastery has been achieved over the action system; rhythmic alpha-type waves now about 8 c.p.s.

10 years to 12 years	EEG record is somewhat of higher frequency than adult's: about 11 c.p.s.
from 12 years on	EEG reveals the adult pattern of alpha activity at a frequency of about 10 c.p.s.

In the normal relaxed infant, rhythmic waves appear in the electroencephalogram after 3 months of age, initially from the occipital (visual) area of the brain. At first, the waves are slow, of low frequency, only about 4 cycles per second. But the frequency increases progressively with age until sometime before the end of the twelfth year when the adult frequency of about 10 cycles per second becomes stabilized.

The stages in psychosexual development

age

Oral

0–1 Primary narcissistic phase—first three months (ca.)—sucking; no distinction between self and environment; psychic energy totally cathected in the self.
Intermediate phase—three to six months (ca.)—pre-objectal—vague, fragmentary differentiation between self and environment; social smile, hand regard, hand to mouth, learning to wait.
Objectal phase—six to 18 months (ca.)—sucking and biting; infant discriminates strangers; establishment of the libidinal object; fusion of the libidinal and aggressive drives onto the object by end of first year.

1–2 Distinction between the I and the NOT I.
Object constancy—the object ceases to be interchangeable—inner image of object.

Anal

2–3 Ambivalence: clinging/controlling love object; retention/elimination of stool.
Natural resistance to habit-training and pleasure in evacuation to be exchanged for compensatory offer of adult approval.
(Method of habit-training may influence character traits—stubbornness, tenderness.)
Mother's absence can be tolerated for longer periods but needs to know she is available.
Mobility greatly increased. Motor drive dominates behavior as the child progresses rapidly in mastering the action system. "The skilled (ego) and the pleasure-seeking (id) aspects of motility reinforce each other" (Mittelman, 1954).

Phallic

3–4 Awareness of sex differences. Assumes sex role. Genitalia strongly cathected.
Intrusion by physical or verbal attack, more common in boys.
Girls aware of lack of penis, tend to attract, receive. Sex play among children.

4–7 Ambivalent feelings towards parent of same sex. Romantic attachment towards parent of other sex, and frustration resulting from inability to compete successfully with same-sex parent for possession of love object. Oedipus and Electra complexes may generate guilt feelings.

Latency

7–12 Much of libido is diverted from genital zone to social ends (peer relations, learning, hobbies, games); sublimation. Temporary resolution of Oedipus and Electra complexes during this 5-6 year lull.

The stages in psychosocial development

age

Basic Trust

0–1 Resolution of the conflict of trust vs. mistrust is the first task of the ego.
Under favorable conditions of affection and object constancy, the infant by the end of the first year will tolerate mother's leaving his perceptual field, knowing that she will return as she has been doing all along. This is a basic stage upon which widening social relations will have their firm foundation. A prime element is the quality rather than the quantity of the mother/infant interaction.

1–2 Mother has become "an inner certainty as well as an outer predictability." Out of sight is not out of mind.

Autonomy, Sense of

2–3 During this period, the child is faced with the task of resolving the conflict between self-assertion and parental control. This is also a task for parents. They will be a positive influence if they encourage independence within a safe framework that does not suppress. Habit-training should aim at self-regulation. Unwise attempts to control the child's assertiveness may instill feelings of shame and doubt, with loss of self-esteem.
Willpower.

Initiative, Sense of

3–4 The child is "on the make" and experiences pleasure in attack and conquest.
Boys tend to be "intrusive" in activity and speech; girls tend to be "catching."
Develop relationships with peers. Identification with same-sex parent.
Conscience is developing. Parents' task is to prevent guilt feelings.

4–7 The child is ready to learn, eager to cooperate constructively with peers.
The Oedipal stage results in "a moral sense restricting the horizon of the permissible."
Ideal adults replace fairy tale heroes.
Parent should set the example and not disillusion the child by hypocritical behavior.
Direction and purpose.

Industry

7–12 Oedipal conflicts are temporarily subdued as the child now is ready and eager to learn from adults and older children. In our culture, school and teachers play a major role in guiding and providing the child with the academic and technological skills in preparation for the "greatest number of all possible careers."
Satisfaction is derived from doing things with others and from making things well.
Destructive criticism and discrimination are particularly damaging influences during this time; they are likely to produce feelings of inadequacy and inferiority. A poor preparation for the next stage of adolescent turmoil and search for an identity.

The stages in cognitive development

age

Sensori-Motor

0–1 Reflexive, undifferentiated, atavistic responses to internal and external stimuli: sucking, grasping, Moro reflex, postural patterns. (first month)
Reflex activity accommodates to the environment as coordination is gradually achieved between sense and motion: smell and sucking, eye-hand coordination. (1 to 4 months)

Movements are becoming goal-directed and increasingly under intentional control: reaching and manipulating, transferring objects from hand to hand. (4 to 8 months)

Purposeful, means-end behavior as control extends distally over trunk so that infant can now sit and free hands for manipulation which is now more skillful: control over radial fingers, pincer grasp; plucks string to secure an attached toy that is out of direct reach. (8 to 12 months)

1–2 The infant thinks and reasons motorically; not as easily distracted for now out of sight is not so readily out of mind. Concept of object permanence. (12 to 24 months)

Rapidly developing expressive language.

Pre-operational

2–4 Preconceptual phase.

Beginning to function symbolically. Language symbols play an increasingly prominent role.

Child is egocentric; thought is distorted by feelings; the child's thinking is "transductive" (categorizes on the basis of only a single characteristic; things belong together because they are together in time and/or space. Relationships are based on irrelevant traits leading thereby to false cause-effect concepts).

4–7 Intuitive phase.

Increased symbolic functioning but still egocentric.

Beginning to classify on more meaningful trait but still on the basis of one trait.

Learning to deal with number concepts; can count and tell the sum.

Thought is still dominated by perception. The child is deceived by irrelevant changes in shape.

Concrete Operations

7–12 As the child gradually becomes less dependent upon his perceptual field, he is able to classify on the basis of general, less concrete aspects. An apple will be thought of as a fruit rather than as something one eats. Thought is now logical.

Able to reverse numbers. (Reversibility is "the capacity to carry out the same action in both directions while being aware that it is the same action" (Piaget, 1957).)

Concepts of conservation of quantity and weight. Beginning to see himself in the other's place (can tell right and left hand of person sitting opposite).

The stages in language development

age

Pre-Linguistic

0–1 **Birth-cry:** an atavism, unconscious, automatism, involuntary, of survival value; the species crying out for its helpless descendant. Phylogenetic.

Ontogenesis: the cry is in response to auditory, tactile, visual, or other sensory experience. Pleasurable reaction (smiling) at first to anyone's full-face approach; after 4 months, as the mother's face is recognized, smiling and laughter are elicited in response to her face preferably, while vowel sounds become more varied. By 6–7 months, polysyllabic vowels and probably an "m-m-m" sound. By 8–9 months, lallation (da-da, baba) uttered as playful sounds, unrelated to persons or things; these sounds are also produced imitatively. ***Inner language*** is manifested by the child's meaningful, adaptive responses and nonverbal communication. During the second half of the first year, ***receptive language*** is being acquired: the infant responds to name and to "no-no," may clap hands and wave bye-bye on request by 9–10 months.

1–2 *Expressive language* develops rapidly after the first year. "Mama" and "dada" or "papa" are used meaningfully. Scribble speech (jargon) parallels the child's delight in kinesthetic scribbling. Words are combined to express action.

2–3 By age two, 3-word sentences are commonly used. Pronouns, particularly "I" and "me," are a prominent feature of verbal usage. There are frequent monologues. Conversation with other children consists mainly in a clash of affirmations, with no account being taken of the other's view. Speech and understanding are egocentric. Reasons given are often reduced to a solitary and final "because." Negation is a dominant feature of behavior and speech. "I don't know" or "I can't" is often used mechanically, when a little encouragement will show that the child *can*. Vocabulary is increasing at an impressive rate. Sentences never heard before are created. Speech reflects the natural egocentricity of these years. Concepts are understood in concrete terms.

3–4 A tricycle, a football, and/or a doll are preferred by far to life, liberty, and the pursuit of happiness. Asked, "What do we do with our eyes?" The child replies, "we close them." Asked, "What do we do with our ears?" He replies "we pull them." (It is not until age five that children are expected to tell the function of both the eyes and the ears.) Children can tell whether they are girls or boys but will ascribe their sex to length of hair, items of clothing, or just "because."

4–7 The adult will be hard put to find appropriate answers to the many "why" and "how" and "what" questions. Articulation loses its infantile quality. The child's vivid imagination finds expression in statements that have no factual basis. The child is becoming aware of how other children feel and is beginning to respond to what others say as egocentricity diminishes and altruism tentatively makes its appearance. Language mirrors
7–12 thought in its development from the concrete to the abstract. It can now express ideas and it can also act upon them. It can express emotional attitudes. It can serve to communicate and to dissimulate.

The stages in drawing behavior

age

The Infant Does Not Draw

0–1 Presented with a crayon, the infant of 3 months will reach for it with his eyes but will be unable to grasp it until 5 months of age. The crayon is examined as eye-hand coordination develops; it is transferred from hand to hand at 6–7 months and brought to mouth. Hand-to-mouth reaction is one of the dominant patterns during the first year.

Kinesthetic Drawing

1–2 The first scribbles are seen at about 15 months; mostly zig-zag, roughly horizontal.

At first the crayon is held crudely in the fist; gradually, the index will guide it.

2–3 As the infant nears age 2, other configurations, lines and arcs will be added to the repertory, but the dominant feature of this period is still the delight in watching movement leave its marks on the paper (preferably on the wall).

By age 3, whirls, coils, and eventually discrete circles predominate. The child seems to be fascinated by the circle and, indeed, this is the simplest pattern, the basic form in nature as it is in the child's perceptual and conceptual development.

Discovery

3–4 A breakthrough occurs when the child suddenly realizes that the circle suggests a relationship to something in visual reality: probably a head. The child has made a symbol. There will be backslidings into the earlier scribbling stage but drawings will become increasingly representational in intent. A circle with protruding lines will symbolize a person. People will be the child's favorite object of graphic representation, just as they are to an overwhelming degree in life.

Representational Drawing

4–7 As the writing instrument comes under improved control, and,
as perception and concept mature, drawing becomes increas-
ingly expressive of what the child knows. The drawing may be
imbued with feelings, particularly when it represents the fam-
ily. Graphic expression of the family is highly subjective and
tells more about the artist than about the object represented.
This is the stage of ***intellectual realism*** as distinct from the next
stage of ***visual realism*** during which the child attempts to draw
what the eye can actually see. Accordingly, transparencies
(people seen through walls, legs through trousers) will no longer
characterize drawings. Heads will no longer dominate the figure
but will be drawn more in visual proportion. By 9 or 10, full-
face will tend to give way to profile representation. The influ-
ence of environmental pressures will be reflected in the draw-
ings. These will tend to be less expressive of the child's individ-
7–12 uality as conformism takes over. With the approach of
adolescence and the development of the critical sense, drawing
will be replaced by other more satisfying forms of self-expres-
sion. The gifted will persevere. This decline of interest in active
participation in the visual arts does not seem to be culturally
determined. It has been observed in the youth of many nations.

Bibliography

ALPERT, A.: Reversibility of pathological fixations associated with maternal deprivation in infancy. *Psychoan. Study Child.* 4:69–185. New York: International Universities Press, 1959.

ALPERT, A.: Institute on programs for children without families. *J. Amer. Acad. Child Psychiat.* 4:165–166, 1965.

ARNHEIM, R.: *Art and Visual Perception.* Berkeley: University of California Press, 1954.

ARNHEIM, R.: *Visual Thinking.* Berkeley: University California Press, 1969.

BAKWIN, H.: Deviant gender-role behavior in children: Relation to homosexuality. *Pediatrics.* 41:620–630, 1968.

BARRON, F. X.: Creativity in children, in *Child Art: The Beginnings of Self-Affirmation.* (H. P. Lewis, ed.) Berkeley: Diablo Press, 1973.

BENDER, L.: The drawing of a man in chronic encephalitis in children. *J. Nervous and Mental Dis.* 40:277–286. 1940.

BILLER, H. B.: Father absence and the personality development of the male child. *Devel. Psychol.* 2:181–201, 1970.

BLOOM, L.: *Language Development: Form and Function in Emerging Grammars.* Cambridge, Mass.: M. I. T. Press, 1970.

BROWN, R.: Development of the first language in the human species. *American Psychologist.* 28, 2, 1973.

BROWN, R. and BELLUGI, U.: Three processes in the child's acquisition of syntax. *Harvard Educ. Review,* 1964, 34:133–151.

BUCK, J. N.: The H-T-P Test. *J. Clin. Psychol.* 1948, 4:151–159.

BUROS, O. K. (ed.): *Seventh Mental Measurements Yearbook.* Highland Park, N.J.: Gryphon Press. 1970. 1630–1631.

BURNS, R. C. & KAUFMAN, S. H.: *Kinetic Family Drawings.* New York: Brunner/Mazel, 1970.

BURNS, R. C. & KAUFMAN, S. H. *Actions, Styles and Symbols in Kinetic Family Drawings.* New York: Brunner/Mazel, 1972.

CHOMSKY, N.: *Aspects of the Theory of Syntax.* Cambridge, Mass.: M.I.T. Press, 1965.

CHOMSKY, N.: Recent contributions to the theory of innate ideas. Boston Studies in the Philosophy of Science, Vol. III, *Proceedings of the Boston Colloquium for the Philosophy of Science,* The Netherlands: D. Reidel, 1964–1966.

CRELIN, E.S.: *Functional Anatomy of the Newborn.* New Haven: Yale Univ. Press, 1973.

D'AMICO, V.: Questions and answers about teaching art, in *Child Art: the Beginnings of Self-Affirmation.* (H. P. Lewis, ed.) Berkeley: Diablo Press, 1973.

DÉCARIE, T. GOUIN.: *Intelligence and Affectivity in Early Childhood.* New York: Intern. Univ. Press, 1965.

DENNIS, W.: *Group Values through Children's Drawings.* New York: J. Wiley, 1966.

DESPERT, J. L.: *The Inner Voices of Children.* New York: Brunner/Mazel, 1975.

DI LEO, J. H.: Developmental evaluation of very young infants, in *Exceptional Infant.* Vol. 1. New York: Brunner/Mazel, 1967.

DI LEO, J. H.: Early detection of developmental disorders, in *Learning Disabilities: Implications for a Responsible Society.* (D. Kronick, ed.) Chicago: Developmental Learning Materials, 1969.

DI LEO, J. H.: *Physical Factors in Growth and Development.* New York: Teachers College Press, 1970.

DI LEO, J. H.: *Young Children and Their Drawings.* New York: Brunner/Mazel, 1970.

DI LEO, J. H.: The special needs of the adopted child. *Medical Insight.* 1973, 5:34–41 (a).

DI LEO, J. H.: *Children's Drawings as Diagnostic Aids.* New York: Brunner/Mazel, 1973 (b).

DI LEO, J. H.: Effects of early malnutrition on structure and function: The case for secondary prevention, in *Handbook of Learning Disabilities.* (R. E. Weber, ed.) Englewood Cliffs, N.J.: Prentice-Hall, 1974.

DOUGLAS, J. W. B.: Early hospital admissions and later disturbances of behavior and learning. *Devel. Med. Child Neurol.* 1975, 17:456–480.

ENG, H.: *The Psychology of Children's Drawings.* (2nd ed.) London: Routledge & Kegan Paul, 1954.

ERIKSON, E. H.: *Childhood and Society.* New York: Norton, 1950.

FREUD, A., & BURLINGHAM, D.: *Infants Without Families.* New York: Intern. Univ. Press, 1944.

FREUD, S.: *A General Introduction to Psychoanalysis.* New York: Doubleday, Garden City, 1943.

GESELL, A.: *Infancy and Human Growth.* New York: Macmillan, 1929.

GESELL, A. and AMATRUDA, C. S.: *Developmental Diagnosis,* 3rd ed. (H. Knobloch and B. Pasamanick, eds.). New York: Harper Medical, 1974.

GESELL, A., ILG, F. L., AMES, L. B. and RODELL, J. L.: *Infant and Child in the Culture of Today.* New York: Harper & Row, 1974.

GESELL, A., and ILG, F. L.: *The Child from Five to Ten.* New York: Harper & Row, 1946.

GOODENOUGH, F. L.: *Measurement of Intelligence by Drawings.* New York: World Book Co., 1926.

HAMMER, E. F.: Guide for qualitative research with the H-T-P. *J. Genet. Psychol.* 1954, 51:41–60.

HARRIS, D. B.: *Children's Drawings as Measures of Intellectual Maturity.* New York: Harcourt, Brace & World, 1963.

HARROWER, M.: *Appraising Personality: The Use of Psychological Tests in the Practice of Medicine.* New York: Norton, 1952.

ILLINGWORTH, R. S.: *The Normal Child.* (5th ed.) Baltimore: Williams & Wilkins, 1972.

JIANOU, I.: *Brancusi.* New York: Tudor Publ. Co., 1963.

JUNG, C. G.: *Analytical Psychology: Its Theory and Practice.* London: Routledge and Kegan Paul, 1968.

KAY, P.: Psychoanalytic theory of development in childhood and preadolescence, in *Handbook of Child Psychoanalysis.* (B. B. Wolman, ed.) New York: Van Nostrand Reinhold, 1972.

KELLOG, R.: *The Psychology of Children's Art.* New York: Random House, 1967.

KERSCHENSTEINER, D. G.: *Die Entwicklung der zeichnerischen Begabung.* Munich: Gerber, 1905.

LANCET, The (editorial) Children in hospital and after. vol. II for 1975. No. 7936, p. 649.

LANSING, K. M.: *Art, Artists, and Art Education.* New York: McGraw-Hill, 1969.

LENNEBERG, E. H.: *Biological Foundations of Language.* New York: Wiley, 1967.

LENNEBERG, R. N.: On explaining language. *Science,* 1969, No. 3880, 164:635–643.

LEVINSTEIN, S.: *Kinderzeichnungen bis zum 14 Lebensjahr.* Leipzig: R. Voigtlander Verlag, 1905.

LEWIS, H. P. (ed.) *Child Art: The Beginnings of Self-Affirmation.* Berkeley: Diablo Press, 1973.

LINDSLEY, D. B.: Brain potentials in children and adults. *Science,* 1936, No. 2181, 84: 384.

LINDSLEY, D. B.: Longitudinal study of the occipital alpha rhythm in normal children: Frequency and amplitude standards. *J. Genet. Psychol.* 1939, 55:197–313.

LOWENFELD, B.: Non-visual art, in *Child Art: The Beginnings of Self-Affirmation.* (H. P. Lewis, ed.) Berkeley: Diablo Press, 1973.

LOWENFELD, V. and BRITTAIN, W. L.: *Creative and Mental Growth.* (5th ed.) New York: Macmillan, 1970.

LUQUET, G. H.: *Les Dessins d'un Enfant: Étude psychologique.* Paris: Librairie Félix Alcan, 1913.

LYSTAD, M.: *A Child's World.* Rockville, Md.: Inst. Mental Health, 1974.

MACHOVER, K.: *Personality Projection in the Drawing of the Human Figure.* Springfield: C C Thomas, 1949.

MAHLER, M. S.: On child psychosis and schizophrenia: Autistic and symbiotic infantile psychoses. *Psychoan. Study Child,* 7:286–305, New York: Intern. Univ. Press, 1952.

MCCARTHY, D.: Language development in children, in *Manual of Child Psychology* (L. Carmichael, ed.). 2nd ed., New York: Wiley, 1954.

MCHUGH, A. F.: Children's figure drawings in neurotic and conduct disturbances. *J. Clin. Psychol.* 22: 219–221, 1966.

MINTZBURG, H.: Planning on the left side and managing on the right. *Harvard Business Rev.* 56:49–59, July-Aug. 1976.

MIRSKY, A. F.: Physiological psychology, in *Behavioral Science and Pediatric Practice.* (N. B. Talbot, J. Kagan, and L. Eisenberg, eds.) Philadelphia: Saunders, 1971.

MITTELMAN, B.: Motility in infants, children, and adults. *Psychoan. Study Child.* IX: 162–178, New York: Intern. Univ. Press, 1954.

MONEY, J.: Psychologic evaluation of the child with intersex problems. *Pediatrics.* 36, 1:51–56, 1965.

MONEY, J., HAMPSON, J. G., and HAMPSON, J. L.: Imprinting and the establishment of gender-role. *Arch. Neurol. & Psychiat.* 77:333, 1957.

MORTON, M.: *The Arts and the Soviet Child.* New York: Free Press, 1972.

MÜHLE, G.: *Entwicklungspsychologie des zeichnerischen Gestaltens.* Munchen: J. A. Barth, 1955.

MYKLEBUST, H. R.: *Auditory Disorders in Children.* New York: Grune & Stratton, 1954.

NELSON, N. H.: Comprehension of spoken language by normal children as a function of speaking rate, sentence difficulty, and listener age. *Child Devel.* 1976, 47:299–303.

ORNSTEIN, R.: *The Psychology of Consciousness.* San Francisco: W. H. Freeman, 1975.

PIAGET, J.: *The Origins of Intelligence in Children.* New York: Norton, 1952.

PIAGET, J.: *The Construction of Reality in the Child.* New York: Basic Books, 1954.

PIAGET, J.: *The Language and Thought of the Child.* Cleveland: World Publ. Co. Meridian Books, 1955.

PIAGET, J., and INHELDER, B.: *Mental Imagery in the Child.* New York: Basic Books, 1971.

PIKLER, E.: Some contributions to the study of the gross motor development of children. *J. Genet. Psychol.* 1968, 113:27–39.

RAPAPORT, D.: *Organization and Pathology of Thought.* New York: Columbia Univ. Press, 1951.

READ, H.: *Art and Society.* New York: Schocken Books, 1966.

REICHLE, J. E., LONGHURST, T. H., and STEPANICH, L.: Verbal interaction in mother-child dyad. *Devel. Psychol.* 1976, 12:273–277.

RICCI, C.: *L'Arte dei Bambini.* Bologna: Zanichelli, 1887.

ROSENBLOOM, L. and HORTON, M. E.: The maturation of fine prehension in young children. *Devel Med. Child Neurol.* 1971, 13:3–8.

RUBIN, W.: Klee's cat and bird. *Bulletin Museum Modern Art,* Spring 1976. New York.

SCHEIBEL, M. E. and SCHEIBEL, A. B.: Some neural substrates of postnatal development. *Child Devel. Research,* vol. 1 New York: Russell Sage Found., 1964.

SCHILDER, P.: *The Image and Appearance of the Human Body.* New York: Intern. Univ. Press, 1950.

SCOTT, J. P.: Critical periods in behavioral development. *Science,* 138:949–958, 1962.

SPITZ, R.: *The First Year of Life.* New York: Intern. Univ. Press, 1965.

SWENSEN, C. H.: Empirical evaluation of human figure drawings: 1957–1966. *Psychol. Bulletin.* 1968, 70:20–44.

TOKER, E.: Psychiatric aspects of cardiac surgery in a child. *J. Amer. Acad. Child Psychiat.* Jan. 1971, 10:176–182.

TRACY, F. and STIMPFL, J.: *The Psychology of Childhood.* Boston: Heath & Co., 1909.

WERNER, H. and KAPLAN, E.: The Acquisition of Word Meanings: A developmental study. Monograph vol. XV, No. 51, 1950. *Soc. Res. Child Devel.*

WINICK, M.: Nutrition and cell growth. *Nutr. Rev.,* 1968, 26:195–197.

WOHLWILL, J. F.: From Perception to Inference: A dimension of cognitive development. Monograph No. 83, vol. 27, 1962, *Soc. Res. Child Devel.*

WOLMAN, B. B.: Psychoanalytic theory of infantile development, in *Handbook of Psychoanalysis.* New York: Van Nostrand Reinhold, 1972.

Index of Names

Index of Subjects